Contexts

Contexts

Meaning, Truth, and the Use of Language

Stefano Predelli

OXFORD
UNIVERSITY PRESS

Great Clarendon Street, Oxford OX2 6DP

Oxford University Press is a department of the University of Oxford.
It furthers the University's objective of excellence in research, scholarship,
and education by publishing worldwide in

Oxford New York

Auckland Cape Town Dar es Salaam Hong Kong Karachi
Kuala Lumpur Madrid Melbourne Mexico City Nairobi
New Delhi Shanghai Taipei Toronto

With offices in

Argentina Austria Brazil Chile Czech Republic France Greece
Guatemala Hungary Italy Japan Poland Portugal Singapore
South Korea Switzerland Thailand Turkey Ukraine Vietnam

Oxford is a registered trade mark of Oxford University Press
in the UK and in certain other countries

Published in the United States
by Oxford University Press Inc., New York

© Stehano Predelli 2005

The moral rights of the author have been asserted
Database right Oxford University Press (maker)

First published 2005

All rights reserved. No part of this publication may be reproduced,
stored in a retrieval system, or transmitted, in any form or by any means,
without the prior permission in writing of Oxford University Press,
or as expressly permitted by law, or under terms agreed with the appropriate
reprographics rights organization. Enquiries concerning reproduction
outside the scope of the above should be sent to the Rights Department,
Oxford University Press, at the address above

You must not circulate this book in any other binding or cover
and you must impose the same condition on any acquirer

British Library Cataloguing in Publication Data

Data available

Library of Congress Cataloging in Publication Data

Data available

Typeset by SPI Publisher Services, Pondicherry, India
Printed in Great Britain
on acid-free paper by
Biddles Ltd, King's Lynn, Norfolk

ISBN 0–19–928173–4   978–0–19–928173–2

1 3 5 7 9 10 8 6 4 2

PREFACE

A sceptical attitude that has been simmering for at least half a century has recently gained considerable popularity among philosophers of language. The conviction that something rotten lies at the very foundation of so-called formal approaches to language, once only timidly whispered by francophone intellectuals and decadent humanists, is now confidently enunciated in (more or less) plain English, and boldly presented to the attention of analytically oriented neighbourhoods.

The customary way of doing semantics has not found among its defenders anything matching the confident tone with which the sceptics put forth their case. To the contrary, the unconvinced and unconvincing responses that have emerged from traditionalist quarters have fuelled the insurgents' enthusiasm: surely, if *that* is all that can be said in favour of the traditional take on natural languages, it is about time to move on. Where one ought to move on to remains unclear: nothing even remotely resembling the scope, elegance, and beauty of the old-fashioned research programme has been presented as an alternative. Still, if the tenability of the traditional edifice did rely on the strategies promoted by its self-proclaimed champions, theoretical poverty would arguably be preferable to the dominance of an inadequate dogma.

The main thesis of this book is that much more is to be said in favour of the established semantic paradigm. The recent sceptical wave, so I argue, is grounded either on false claims or on inconsequential trivialities. But the anti-traditionalists' mistakes are unlikely to be rectified as long as they are echoed by responses which, though superficially critical of the sceptical view, do in fact concede the premises upon which it rests. The problem is not novel: the misunderstandings shared by sceptics and contemporary traditionalists alike may be traced back to a variety of independent assumptions with which the traditional paradigm has all too often been associated. Only a thorough analysis of the conceptions of meaning, truth, and the use of language to which 'formal' semantics is committed may eliminate deep-rooted confusions, and reveal the true explanatory power of the traditional approach.

ACKNOWLEDGEMENTS

I am indebted to David Kaplan and Nathan Salmon, my teachers and mentors at the University of California, who introduced me to the beauties of the traditional paradigm in natural language semantics. Although this book's fervent traditionalism sometimes ends up being at odds with some aspects of their views, the philosophical background assumed in this essay is importantly inspired by their approach to language.

Thanks also to those who had the patience and perseverance to discuss metasemantics with me in the last couple of years. John Perry and Ben Caplan deserve special mention for the charitable attitude with which they listened to my semantic ramblings, and for their ability to present their comments and criticisms in a most productive form. Similar praise goes to the anonymous referees who read this manuscript and made very welcome suggestions for improvements.

Equally fruitful were my exchanges with exponents from the 'enemy camp'. A special token of appreciation goes to François Recanati for the generosity with which he tolerated my stubborn anti-contextualism. A very heartfelt thanks goes to Claudia Bianchi, who helped me better understand the scope and content of the contextualist challenge.

My good friend and colleague Eros Corazza deserves special recognition. Many thanks for his hospitality before and after I moved to Nottingham, for his comments on my work, and for the frequent and always superb dinners at his house. Thank you also to Kent Bach, Stephen Barker, Jonathan Berg, Emma Borg, Herman Cappelen, Robyn Carston, Manuel Garcia-Carpintero, Jon Gorvett, Max Kölbel, Ernie Lepore, John MacFarlane, Genoveva Marti, Stephen Neale, Komarine Romdenh-Romluc, Phillippe Schlenker, Jason Stanley, Alberto Voltolini, Sandro Zucchi, and all those with whom I had the pleasure to discuss questions related to this book's main topic. Last but not least my gratitude goes to Peter Momtchiloff, Rupert Cousens, and OUP for their help and encouragement.

A few paragraphs in this essay are reproductions or slight modifications of passages from some of my published essays. I would like to thank the editors for permission to use material from 'Talk about Fiction', *Erkenntnis*, 46 (1997), 69–77; 'I Am Not Here Now', *Analysis*, 58 (1998), 107–15; 'Utterance, Interpretation, and the Logic of Indexicals', *Mind and Language*, 13/3 (1998), 400–14; 'The Price of Innocent Millianism', *Erkenntnis*, 60 (2004), 335–56; 'The Problem with Token Reflexivity', *Synthese* (forthcoming); 'Think Before You Speak: Utterances and the Logic of Indexicals', *Argumentation* (forthcoming); and 'Painted Leaves, Context, and Semantic Analysis', *Linguistics and Philosophy* (forthcoming).

CONTENTS

Introduction	1
1. Systems and their Inputs	8
2. Systems and Indexes	40
3. The Vagaries of Action	76
4. The Colour of the Leaves	119
5. The Easy Problem of Belief Reports	161
Conclusion	184
Bibliography	188
Index	197

Introduction

It seems reasonable to suppose that the expressions we use as speakers of a language such as English mean something. It is also natural to assume that, under appropriate conditions, the employment of at least some among these expressions achieves effects describable with the help of locutions such as 'true' or 'false'. Finally, it is at least prima facie sensible to hypothesize that there is an interesting connection between these dimensions, and that a philosophically interesting story may be told about the relationship between meaning, truth, and the use of language. An important research programme within linguistics and philosophy of language, sometimes called 'natural language semantics' or 'formal semantics', is grounded on a particular notion of how such a story, or at least an important portion of it, is supposed to go. The aim of the present book is to clarify the understanding of meaning and truth that lies at the basis of the aforementioned programme, to explain how it may be applied to particular instances involving the use of language, and to defend it against an increasingly fashionable sceptical attitude. The projects of clarification and defence are complementary. The critics of the traditional paradigm, so I argue, proceed from incorrect assumptions about its scope and structure. Still, their mistake is understandable: to an important extent, the traditional approach to semantics has been misunderstood even by its foremost defenders, in particular when it comes to the theory of meaning and truth upon which it is grounded.

1. The Plan: Chapters 1–3

The traditional paradigm within formal semantics has generated a multiplicity of different proposals, focused on alternative features of the semantic behaviour of natural languages. In this book I focus on the type of structures that emerged a few decades ago within the debate on so-called indexical languages. Although a variety of alternative approaches would do for my purpose, I concentrate for concreteness' sake on treatments somewhat reminiscent of those developed within the Montagovian tradition, and now typically associated with the work of Hans Kamp, David Kaplan, and David Lewis. As I explain in Chapter 1, formal approaches of this type are specifically interested in certain aspects of contextual dependence: namely, those relevant for the interpretation and evaluation of indexical expressions. Simple indexical expressions, such as 'I' or 'now', refer to distinct items with respect to alternative parameters, say, the person who is speaking or the time of utterance, and they apparently do so in virtue of certain aspects of their conventional meaning. For this reason, the study of languages of this ilk provides a particularly fertile ground for the discussion of the interface between questions of meaning, issues of reference and truth, and at least certain forms of the contextual sensitivity uncontroversially affecting our linguistic interchanges. In particular, according to the classical view, the analysis of this interface reveals important logical properties of certain expressions; that is, it uncovers constructions which, in the traditional parlance, are 'true in virtue of meaning'.

Chapter 1 is devoted to a general and relatively informal explanation of the structures traditionally employed for the analysis of simple linguistic fragments involving indexical expressions. These structures take certain abstract items as input, and yield assignments of truth-values and, consequently, of logical properties and relations. As will emerge later in this essay, widespread mistakes regarding the scope and function of such structures may in part be traced to the formally unobjectionable, but pedagogically misleading choice of certain labels for a variety of the aforementioned parameters. For instance, it is common to refer to the *analysanda* in the project under discussion as 'sentence–context pairs', and to the results with which they are paired as 'truth-conditions'. It is also customary to label the theoretical machinery designed for the assignment of truth-conditions to such pairs as a procedure of 'semantic' compositional interpretation. In order not to prejudge a variety of issues that eventually become of immediate concern in later chapters, I opt for an artificial, deliberately neutral terminology: I thus talk of *interpretive systems* (or, more often, simply *systems*) which, when applied to *clause–index* pairs, yield conclusions of *t-distributions*, i.e., assignments of truth-value at particular *points* of evaluation.

One of the didactic pay-offs for this unwieldy terminology consists in the rather obvious chasm it imposes between the interpretive system's concerns, on the one hand, and, on the other, the questions pertaining to its *application* to the nitty-gritty of everyday language use. Systems assign t-distributions to clause–index pairs, but competent and intelligent speakers are attuned to more tangible dimensions: in particular, to the intuitive truth-values of particular utterances on given occasions. If systems may eventually come to grips with such intuitions and aim at results consonant with them, they may do so only on the assumption of appropriate hypotheses about their interface with the world of daily exchanges—hypotheses pertaining to the clause–index pair adequate for the representation of an utterance, and to the understanding of the system's t-distributional output in truth-conditional terms. In a more pictorial fashion

> utterance
> clause-index $\longrightarrow$ system $\longrightarrow$ t-distribution
>   truth-conditions

The discussion of the 'gaps' between, on the one hand, the system's input (a clause–index pair) and output (a t-distribution), and, on the other hand, the intuitive parameters of semantic analysis (an utterance's truth-conditions), is one of this book's main concerns. In the final sections of Chapter 1, I begin to address the relationship between an utterance—that is, an instance of language use taking place in a given context—and the clause–index pair appropriate for its analysis. Armed with the discussion of such relationship, I critically approach some considerations put forth by the defenders of a fashionable sceptical standpoint having to do with issues such as disambiguation or reference assignment.

In Chapter 2, I continue my discussion of how utterances may be appropriately represented from the interpretive system's point of view. In particular, I focus on the relationship between the *context* in which an utterance takes place and the index involved in its representation. The starting-point for this discussion is provided by rather frivolous cases, having to do with recorded messages and written notes. But the point which these examples help to uncover transcends the not-so-urgent need for a theory of postcards or answering machines. The main conclusion of this chapter is that even some of the foremost defenders of the customary treatment of indexical languages have burdened traditional systems with extraneous assumptions, thereby concealing the view of meaning and truth to which they are truly committed. The methodological gains of my non-traditional labels, in particular my cautious distinction between contexts and indexes, are apparent in this respect. It is indeed advisable, at least at a preliminary stage, that questions related to the parameters selected by the meanings of indexicals be isolated from the assumption that what is being addressed is a context, in the everyday sense of the concrete setting in which an utterance takes place. The relationship between a context and what I call an 'index', namely the collection of items requested by the meaning of the indexicals under analysis, is non-trivial, and should not be prejudged by unwarranted terminological decisions.

Chapter 3 continues the discussion of the relationships between the interpretive system's mechanisms and its application to particular utterances. In agreement with the founding fathers of the traditional treatment of indexical languages, systems of the type sketched in Chapter 1 operate on clause–index pairs; i.e., they evaluate expression-types with respect to appropriate additional parameters. It has, however, occasionally been suggested that an alternative, and possibly more appropriate, approach to indexicality eschews expression-types, in favour of a *reflexive* analysis geared towards their particular exemplars. The motivation behind this suggestion, or at least behind the versions of so-called utterance semantics in which I am interested, is semantic, rather than metaphysical. What is at issue is not the antipathy for abstract instantiables, such as, presumably, types, or the predilection for the everyday concreteness of tokens. The point has rather to do with the aims and scope of a systematic analysis able to yield results for utterances, i.e., with the aims and scope of 'applied interpretive systems'. It is on these terms that I take up the utterance-semanticist's challenge. The conclusion I reach is negative: on an appropriate understanding of meaning and truth, interpretive systems had better steer clear of the structures proposed by token-reflexive approaches.

2. The Plan: Chapters 4–5

Chapters 2 and 3 pursue different themes related to the appropriate *input* for an interpretive system, and to its applications to particular utterances. The discussion of the relationship between clause–index pairs and utterances is important, because systems—namely, procedures that operate on the former—aim at empirical adequacy; i.e., at consistency with pre-theoretic intuitions pertaining to the latter. What is desired, among other things, is that the interpretive system, when supplied a clause–index pair appropriate to a certain utterance u, gives results suitably related to (at least some among) our intuitive verdicts about u. But the interface between the system's theory of meaning and truth, on the one hand, and the treatment of particular instances of language use, on the other, does not only raise questions pertaining to the input on which the former operates. As highlighted by the deliberately artificial terminology I adopt in Chapter 1, what systems yield are results of *t-distributions*. Yet, what our intuitive assessments puts forth are not judgements of truth-values at particular points of evaluation, but conclusions of *truth-conditions*. It is to the analysis of the relationship between t-distributions and truth-conditions—that is, in the figurative jargon introduced above, to the discussion of the second 'gap' separating interpretive systems from everyday intuitions—that Chapter 4 is devoted.

It is here that I return to the fashionable contextualist attacks on traditional structures that I began addressing in Chapter 1. Leaving aside the additional worries briefly addressed there, having to do with reference assignment or ambiguity resolution, the contextualists ground their challenge on the conviction that customary treatments of meaning and truth are empirically inadequate: the view of meaning and truth presupposed in Chapter 1, so it is claimed, often yields incorrect conclusions of truth-conditions. I disagree: once the aim and scope of a traditional interpretive system are properly understood, the intuitively required truth-conditional outcomes are perfectly consistent with that system's t-distributional results.

As this preliminary summary of the first four chapters indicates, this essay's main concern is of a 'metasemantic' nature:

what I address are the philosophical and theoretical commitments of treatments of a particular type, in particular their commitment to certain views about meaning and truth. Yet, the discussion of these general issues is of relevance not only from the point of view of the assessment of an influential research programme, but also for a variety of questions 'internal' to it. If my considerations in the first four chapters of this essay are correct, the traditional approach to meaning and truth has been misunderstood, to varying extents, not only by the foremost contextualist sceptics, but also by many who take a friendlier attitude towards it. Unsurprisingly, this misunderstanding has affected the treatment of a multitude of problems that typically occupy traditional semanticists in their everyday toil, regardless of their reactions to one or another among the challenges to the core assumptions within their paradigm. I attempt to substantiate this contention by example. One will have to suffice, but this lack is at least partially compensated by the fact that what I confront in the final chapter of this essay is one of the most discussed semantic problems of recent decades: the treatment of attitude reports and of singular terms occurring within them. Chapter 5 argues for the conclusion that, once the aims and structure of the interpretive system are properly understood, the problem raised by occurrences of singular terms within attitude reports is an 'easy' one, in the sense that it does not require the negation of any among the most straightforward views regarding reference, attitude predicates, complementizers, and the like.

Chapter 1
Systems and their Inputs

ACCORDING to the textbook definition, semantics has to do with certain relations between the (or at least some among the) expressions in a language, on the one hand, and typically extralinguistic objects, on the other. The standard example of a semantically interesting relationship is that between a name and its referent: a linguistic item such as 'Felix' has apparently something to do with Felix, a cat. This relatively unproblematic example of a semantic feature and of the extralinguistic items it targets is, however, typically accompanied by a list of other less straightforward instances: predicates are semantically related to classes of individuals, sentences to truth-values, and, more generally, expressions of all sorts get paired with non-linguistic entities of a peculiar type, their meanings.[1]

To the uninitiated, this characterization of the topic of semantic inquiry may seem surprising, and not only for the blasé inclusion among the 'things in the world' of relatively uncommon objects such as classes or truth-values. In particular, one

[1] David Crystal, for instance, explains that (philosophical) semantics studies the 'relations between linguistic expressions and the phenomena in the world to which they refer, and considers the conditions under which such expressions can be said to be true or false', but proceeds to indicate its scope as 'the study of the meaning of expressions' (Crystal 1991: 310).

may be taken aback by the rather swift mention of meanings side by side with reference and truth, and may require a more detailed explanation of the relationship which these parameters bear to utterances of given expressions under particular conditions. Perhaps there eventually turns out to be a field of inquiry interestingly devoted both to the study of an expression's meaning *and* to the analysis of its relationship to, say, a cat, a class of felines, or a truth-value. Perhaps, such a field of enquiry eventually yields some illuminating conclusions pertaining to the truth-values of particular utterances. But, so the unbiased reader may complain, what one needs is at least a preliminary story of an interesting, systematic interface between truth, meaning, and the use of language.

Still, a moment of more or less commonsensical reflection ought to give at least a preliminary picture of what such a relationship may amount to. Expressions are apparently endowed with a certain meaning by virtue of (possibly among other things) the arbitrary conventions regulating the language to which they belong. It is the (or at least a) function of that meaning to determine, perhaps together with other elements, semantic relations and properties such as those mentioned above. Surely, if the English predicate 'is on the mat' turns out to be associated with the class of objects on the mat, this must have at least something to do with the fact that 'is on the mat' in English means what it does, and not something else. By the same token, if one feels at all inclined to talk of meaning for proper names, it is the meaning of 'Felix', or at least the set of conventions regulating its use on appropriate occasions, which determines that it refers to Felix, rather than to its owner. And on the assumption that the English sentence 'Felix is on the mat' is suitably related to falsehood with respect to how things actually are with the cat, it appears to be an obvious outcome of 'not' meaning what it does that the English sentence 'Felix is not on the mat' turns out to be true. Among the many things that

Systems and their Inputs ~ 9

meaning seems to do is that it provides contributions of immediate relevance for the conditions under which certain expressions relate to certain entities and, ultimately, for the conditions under which sentences relate to truth or falsehood. Similarly, it would seem that the employment of those expressions in suitable circumstances ought to be somewhat interestingly related to such effects: given how things are with Felix, utterances of 'Felix is not on the mat' are to be evaluated as true, precisely on the basis of (perhaps among other things) the aforementioned regularities affecting 'Felix', 'is on the mat', and 'not'.

Regardless of whether my label of 'commonsensical' is at all appropriate for the preliminary hints in the previous paragraph, the resulting picture is sufficiently imprecise to be hardly satisfying to an analytically inclined audience. One version of the approach I just sketched, however, has been developed into a rather rigorous and influential view of semantics, and into a parallel philosophically loaded theory of the relationship between meaning and truth. Historically, this view was inspired to a large extent by the methods and procedures employed in the analysis of artificial systems, typically the symbolic systems developed for the study of certain logically interesting structures. For this and other reasons, it is often presented with the help of a formally rigorous apparatus, one that occasionally bears more than a passing resemblance to structures in mathematical logic and model theory. Accordingly, friends and foes of such an approach tend to refer to it as 'formal semantics'. Since the extent to which views of meaning and truth are presented with the help of a formal apparatus is not immediately relevant for my purpose, I occasionally settle for the equally widespread label of 'natural language semantics'. And since it is a view which, according to its defenders and opposers alike, has gained considerable footing, I also often refer to it as the 'traditional' view. This book is devoted to the analysis of what the traditional view entails about meaning, truth, and the use of language, and to the defence of the resulting picture against a variety of misunderstandings and criticisms.

1. A Rough First Sketch

In this section, I provide a cursory (and, to a certain extent, temporary) summary of the structures customarily employed within the traditional analysis of the relationship between meaning and truth. A non-indifferent portion of the debate surrounding the tenability and adequacy of such constructions often involves terminological discussions: in particular the debate pertaining to the scope and limits of what may legitimately be called *semantic* inquiry. The structures I am about to present (and more complex developments of them) are typically the sort of objects with which so-called natural language semanticists are concerned, and would seem to deserve descriptions in terms of 'semantic evaluation', 'semantic interpretation', and the like. Still, in a cautious attempt not to prejudge the issue with possibly misleading terminological assumptions, I eschew the 's'-word in favour of a more neutral terminology. I settle for *(interpretive) system*.[2] The analysis of the exact relationship between systems, on the one hand, and the presumably semantically interesting *analysanda* (utterances, sentences, etc.) and outcomes (truth-conditions, validity, etc.), on the other, is one of the main topics of this essay.

Languages such as English contain simple expressions—as a very rough first approximation, individual English words—which may occur within larger constructions according to the rules of English syntax. It is the responsibility of the interpretive system to provide hypotheses pertaining to the meaning of these simple

---

[2] Elsewhere I referred to systems as '(interpretive) modules' (see e.g. Predelli 2004).

expressions, and to the effects generated by combining them into more complex expressions. Once this procedure reaches the level of sentences, the results it yields are items appropriately involving a *truth*-value, i.e., for the purpose of this essay, either truth or falsehood.

Of course, the system's task is not that of directly associating sentences with truth-values *tout court*. Whether 'Felix is on the mat' is true or not depends not only upon the regularities governing the English language, but also upon the fact of the matter regarding the relationship between Felix and the mat. What the system aims at determining is not the history of Felix's movements, but rather the systematic manner in which the value for 'Felix is on the mat' co-varies with alternative decisions regarding who is where. Importantly different proposals have been put forth, pertaining to the structure and make-up of the factors with respect to which truth-value assignments should be relativized. It may, for instance, be wondered whether whatever provides a decision regarding Felix's position should also take a stand with respect to a variety of unrelated questions—that is, roughly speaking, whether it is supposed to supply a *total* possible history of the world. Or, to cite another among many other issues, it may be debated whether the appropriate parameter ought to include a temporal dimension: truth with respect to any time t and possible course of history h as long as Felix is lying on the mat in h at t.[3] Be that as it may, it is worth noting that, notwithstanding the pedagogical charm of the aforementioned descriptions, the system's austere structure remains indifferent to the factual details of Felix's biography. What the system aims at yielding are results of truth-value with respect to parameters

---

[3] On the semantic role of *partial* situations, see the considerable literature in the tradition of so-called situation semantics, as originated in Barwise and Perry 1983. For a discussion of the relativization of interpretation to a temporal parameter (and related questions pertaining to the treatment of temporal operators) see e.g. Richard 1981 and 1982.

which, possibly unlike mere descriptions of Felix's whereabouts, provide a *definite* answer to the issue which is apparently of relevance for this purpose: is the being-on relationship such that Felix is the appropriate *relatum* with respect to the mat? These rather cryptic remarks pertaining to the parameters' austerity will be more closely assessed later, in Chapter 4. For the moment, it is advisable that I settle once again for a deliberately artificial label, that of a *point* of evaluation: a sentence, for instance, will be said to be true 'at' (or 'with respect to') a point, but false with respect to another. Later in this essay, the relationships between points in general and the popular understanding of them as 'possible worlds' will be scrutinized more closely.[4]

In the preliminary sketch I have provided, traditional systems involve hypotheses regarding the meaning of simple expressions and the effects achieved by their combination into more complex structures. On the basis of such hypotheses, they eventually yield a certain verdict for sentences: namely, an outcome of truth-values at particular points. In what follows, I refer to such an assignment of truth-values in relation to alternative points of evaluation with the help of the deliberately non-committal label *t-distribution*.

The preliminary, simple-minded version of the traditional approach that I have sketched thus far is, however, unsatisfactory for a variety of reasons. Some, discussed in the remainder of this chapter, are of particular relevance for my purpose.

---

[4] Note incidentally that, if the relativization of truth-value to points is to yield any informative account of the relationship between meaning and truth, the type of information provided by a point may not renegotiate the very meaning of the expressions in question. It is obviously the case that there are points with respect to which 'English is being spoken' or ' "Felix" names Felix' turns out to be false. But the existence of these points is irrelevant when it comes to an assessment of 'Felix is on the mat' at *k*: regardless of the possibility that, according to *k*, 'is on' means what 'eats' means in English, 'Felix is on the mat' turns out to be true at *k* as long as Felix is on the mat, and false if he is not.

2. Clause–Index Pairs

One important assumption regarding the structure of systems is its insistence that the items upon which they operate be assigned univocally the type of result they eventually yield. On the assumption that systems render outcomes of t-distribution, it must be the case that, given a particular input, at most one t-distribution is obtained—in fact, in the simple structures I consider, exactly one. It follows that if the system is supposed to yield appropriate results regarding the objects it studies, these must be the kind of objects that bear such a relationship to t-distributions. Given a few further assumptions, it is a consequence of this approach that English *sentences* (and, more generally, English expressions) are not the kind of objects that systems may take into consideration.

One of the reasons for this conclusion is the fact that English is what is usually called an *ambiguous* language. Perhaps the simplest source of such ambiguity is the phenomenon of *lexical* ambiguity: expressions that are written and spelled the same way intuitively have distinct semantic profiles.[5] My use of 'that is an expensive bill' as I discuss my reluctance to finance a prospective piece of legislation apparently instantiates the same sentence-type as your

---

[5] This paragraph remains deliberately non-committal with respect to certain well-known philosophical issues surrounding lexical ambiguity, and somewhat hazy in the choice of the terminology most appropriate for the description of the cases under discussion. One of the issues I ought to mention, if only to set it aside, is that of whether the aforementioned examples are best described as instances involving *one* expression endowed with two semantic profiles or *two* expressions that happen to be spelled and pronounced the same. Still, at least if my approach is on the right track, nothing of relevance for the purpose of this essay hinges on a choice of this matter. For concreteness' sake I often employ the old-fashioned 'expression-type' vocabulary: e.g., the expression-type 'bill' may be employed so as to denote beaks on some occasions and prospective laws on others. A variety of alternative views of word-identity, however, are compatible with the considerations in what follows. (For a different, and from my point of view more interesting, kind of issue surrounding the semantic employment of types, see the debate discussed in Ch. 3).

use of 'that is an expensive bill' while refusing to purchase a costly parrot. Yet, intuitively, different truth-values may well be appropriate for the examples in question: for instance, in cases in which the bird is pricey but the proposed law is not. It follows that examples involving ambiguous lexical items are pre-theoretically matched with alternative intuitions of meaning, truth-value, and the like, depending on the appropriate choice of one interpretation or another for the items in question. If systems are to yield definite conclusions, and if they have to bear an appropriate relation to our intuitive verdicts, it seems inevitable that instances of lexical ambiguity undergo a process typically labelled 'disambiguation', and that it is the results of such a process, rather than the sentences to which it applies, that interpretive systems take into consideration.[6]

Similar considerations hold for another well-known type of ambiguity, structural ambiguity. So, for instance, the sentence-type

> The United States President is necessarily born in the United States

may be interpreted as providing the true indication that, due to the necessities of the American Constitution, whoever is elected President is a native, or as conveying the false claim that the man

---

[6] The choice of uncontroversial examples of lexical ambiguity is not trivial. The definite article 'the' is sometimes used to denote a unique individual, as in the zoo keeper's utterance of 'The wolf is trying to escape', but sometimes to speak of typical traits of the species itself, as in the ethologist's utterance of 'The wolf takes a mate for life' (I borrow this example from Kamp and Reyle 1993). Yet, it would be at least premature to suppose that 'the' is an instance of lexical ambiguity on a par with 'bill'. These examples are of course negotiable: I may after all turn out to be wrong with respect to both 'the' and 'bill'. Fortunately, nothing in what follows depends on the difficult issues surrounding generic uses of 'The wolf takes a mate for life', and, more generally, the semantic profile of 'the'. As for 'bill', I continue uncritically to assume that it is a prototypical case of accidental lexical ambiguity. The reader equipped with a theory of the systematic relations between beak-denoting and law-related uses of the word is invited to substitute for my examples whatever she deems to be appropriate.

who happens to be President could not have been born abroad. This apparent duality of content must presumably stem (i) from the fact that the aforementioned sentence may result from distinct syntactic processes, and (ii) from the interpretive system's sensitivity to such a distinction. It follows that, taking for granted certain demands on the relationship between the input and output of customary systems, the objects of analysis are not English expressions and, ultimately, English sentences, but more complex expression-types (possibly together with other items).

As for lexical ambiguity, customary analyses achieve the desired distinction by means of subscript numerals: 'bill$_1$' and 'bill$_2$' are supposed to reflect the differences between the legislative and ornithological uses of the word. As for structural ambiguity, to cite just a few among many important proposals, appropriate inputs for the system may take the shape of labelled trees, or of bracketed structures such as

[[[Felix]$_N$]$_{NP}$ [is on the mat]$_{VP}$].

Issues of lexical and structural ambiguity are not, in and of themselves, an important target of this essay, and whether my rather simple-minded analyses of 'bill' or 'Felix is on the mat' are at all adequate is a question that has no bearing on the general issues I am about to discuss. What is important, from the methodological point of view, is, rather, the conclusion that, whatever they may be, expressions such as 'bill$_1$' are *not* English words, and structures such as '[[[Felix]$_N$]$_{NP}$ [is on the mat]$_{VP}$]' are *not* English sentences, even though they are presumably interestingly related to their natural language counterparts. (Alternatively: they are English 'Words' and 'Sentences' in some theoretically loaded sense, distinct from the everyday sense in which words and sentences are identified.) Remaining neutral as to the nature of the constructs best suited to being substitutes for sentences, I settle for the label *clause*. As for the nature of the relationship between sentences and clauses, thus far only vaguely indicated by means of locutions such as 'counterpart' or 'substitute', I devote most of section 4 to a discussion of how the system's rarefied inputs may have a bearing *vis-à-vis* the study of actual instances of the use of English expressions.

There is at least one other reason why sentences won't be an adequate input to interpretive systems even remotely suitable for the analysis of meaning and truth in natural languages. Your use of 'That is an expensive bill' while pointing at the Free Lunch Measure, and my rejoinder 'That is an expensive bill' while pointing at the No Tax Proposition intuitively display interestingly different properties, of the type of concern from the system's point of view, even under the assumption that we both use 'bill' in the legislative sense, without concern for beaks. Similarly, the non-ambiguous 'I am hungry' may well be true in your mouth but false when used by me, given one fixed state of affairs regarding our appetites. The reason for such disparity is apparently traceable to the contributions provided by 'that' or 'I' on the basis of their conventional usage: it is a brute fact about English that 'I' and 'that' refer to different individuals on different occasions, respectively (at least more often than not) the person who is talking and an appropriately salient object. This conclusion is relatively uncontroversial: in virtue of its unique meaning, 'I' yields distinct individuals with respect to distinct parameters of an appropriate kind. The customary name for such parameters is 'context': 'I' refers to one individual in a certain context, and to another individual in a different context. There would be no reason to deviate from customary usage were it not that, as I explain in later chapters, such a terminological decision may support indirectly a variety of pernicious misunderstandings of the profile for expressions such as 'I' or 'that', and of their relationships to a particular individual or time. Given that 'I', 'that', and the like are typically referred to as *indexical* expressions, 'index' seems to be a reasonable alternative. It is not pedagogically without its drawbacks either, given that some authors have employed this locution to refer to what I called 'points of evaluation' (see Lewis 1980). Still, once the difference between my use of 'index' and, say, David Lewis's has been explicitly acknowledged, no confusions should arise in what follows. As for the choice of indexicals, I rest satisfied, at least temporarily, with a highly uncontroversial list, including undisputed candidates such as 'I' and 'now', together with 'today', 'here', simple demonstratives such as 'that', and, for reasons that will become apparent later, 'actually'. I return to the discussion of arguments in favour of more surprising instances of indexicality in later chapters. As for the presumed peculiarities of demonstratives, I address some issues in section 6 below, and others in Chapter 2.[7]

In this section I have briefly rehearsed the reasons why traditional interpretive systems focus on artificial items of a particular kind: namely, what I called clauses, coupled with indexes. In what follows I thus refer to the inputs for the interpretive system as *clause–index pairs*. Given a clause–index pair as input, the system proceeds to the assignment of a particular t-distribution: i.e., to the assignment of truth-values relative to alternative points of evaluation. Equivalently, as I sometimes write, the system assigns a truth-value to a clause, with respect to (or at) a point and an index. In the next section, I explain how an interpretive system proceeds to the assignment of certain results to given clause–index pairs.

3. The System

Having alerted the reader to the true nature of the system's input, in this section I proceed to the presentation of its structure following a customary pedagogical strategy: I pretend, for in-

---

[7] For a discussion of a multitude of indexical expressions in languages other than English, see Anderson and Keenan 1985.

stance, that the system, given an index, deals with English expressions, such as the name 'Felix' or the sentence 'Felix isn't on the mat now', rather than employing more precise but cumbersome locutions, such as the system's treatment of [Felix]$_N$ or

[[not]$_{CONN}$[[now]$_O$ [[Felix]$_N$ [is on the mat]$_{VP}$]$_S$]$_S$]$_S$.

The general methodological significance of the fact that, strictly speaking, what is at issue are clauses rather than sentences will return to the foreground in later sections, especially when I discuss the relationships between the system and actual instances of language use, such as utterances of 'Felix isn't on the mat now'.

The fragment that suffices for my purposes is simple. As for the lexicon, I rest satisfied with a few expressions that I treat as singular terms: some proper names, such as 'Felix', indexicals such as 'I' or 'that', and, for simplicity's sake, the definite description 'the mat'.[8] I employ a few transitive and intransitive verbs (or verb-phrases), such as 'is green' or 'is on', the usual connectives 'not', 'and', and 'or', and some sentential operators, 'now', 'necessarily', 'actually', 'always'. I assume (one version or another) of the obvious rules leading to properly formed complex expressions, such as 'is on the mat', 'Felix is on the mat', or 'Felix is not on the mat now'. In the remainder of the book, I occasionally extend my lexicon and syntax silently in an obvious manner, in order to deal with new examples.

As I mentioned above, interpretive systems assign certain values to the expressions under consideration with respect to an index and a point. As for points, I follow for concreteness' sake the rather customary notion that they be interpreted as pairs, consisting of a

---

[8] My treatment of 'the mat' as a singular term is highly suspicious—as is, incidentally, my treatment of the plural 'the leaves' as a name for a certain foliage, when it comes to some examples in Ch. 4. However, nothing of relevance for my aim hinges on this pretence.

time and what is commonly called a (*possible*) *world* (but for comments and important caveats on the role of 'possible worlds' within semantic interpretation, see Chapter 4). Given a language containing the indexical expressions 'I', 'here', 'now', 'actually', and 'that' (the demonstrative), an index is an *n*-tuple containing at least an individual (the 'agent'), a time, a location, a world, and a *demonstratum*. Intuitively, the idea is that, with respect to an index containing John as the agent, 'I' refers to John; but that, with respect to an index containing Mary as the agent, 'I' refers to Mary. And so on, *mutatis mutandis*, for the other cases.[9]

More precisely, the system approaches the aforementioned simple expressions by assigning to them a particular function, one that takes into consideration particular indexes, and yields a result of a particular type. Following David Kaplan, these functions are often called *characters*. As a first approximation, for instance, we may think of the character of 'I' as a function which, given a certain index, returns the index's agent as the appropriate referent. When it comes to non-indexical expressions, such as the name 'Felix', characters are presumably unexciting constant functions: with respect to any index, 'Felix' always refers to Felix. Similarly, continuing with some pedagogical simplifications, the character of the non-indexical verb-phrase 'is green' (ignoring issues of tense) is the constant function that inevitably yields something having to do with greenness, and the character of the non-indexical operator 'not' is the constant function that renders something having to do with negation.[10]

---

[9] It should be noted that, although I usually follow Kaplan 1977 and consider 'now' as a sentential operator, I may occasionally shift to an analysis of 'now' as a singular term denoting times. Nothing of significance results from such duality.

[10] Slightly more precisely, the character for 'Felix' is the function which, for any index i, renders a function f such that, for any point p, $f(p)$ is Felix; and the character for 'is green' (ignoring tense) is the function which, for any i, yields an f such that $f(p)$ is the class of green things in p.

The hypotheses put forth regarding an expression's character are supposed to reflect at least some aspects of its conventional meaning. For instance, on the assumption that what is at issue is the English expression 'I', what must be given is an account consonant with the notion that, in virtue of its meaning, this expression refers to appropriate individuals *vis-à-vis* particular indexes, rather than, say, to the class of green things. This relatively harmless claim, however, does not amount to the questionable notion that the character for an expression *exhausts* the regularities encoded in its meaning. To the contrary, it seems plausible to insist that certain expressions share a character but differ in meaning, in the sense that speakers of the language must be attuned to more than their character in order to employ them competently. It may well be the case, for instance, that 'stomach' and 'belly' share a character, roughly the constant function that yields a particular abdominal region of the human body, notwithstanding the fact that competent English speakers legitimately refuse to use these expressions interchangeably. Be that as it may, characters are intended to encode that portion of an expression's meaning that is of interest from the interpretive system's point of view—i.e., that is relevant with respect to the assignment of semantic values. Since it is this aspect of the traditional approach that is the subject of this study, I proceed under the pretence that 'character' may be used as synonymous with 'meaning'.[11]

The system then proceeds with the assignment of a value to a complex expression, solely on the basis of that expression's structure, and of the values of its components. Take the typical rule for a clause s consisting of an intransitive verb v and a singular term n (writing for brevity's sake 'true (i, w, t)' for 'true with respect to an index i, a world w, and a time t):

---

[11] On character, meaning, and indexicality, see Braun 1994, 1995, and 1996.

> s is true (i, w, t) iff the value of n at i and w, t belongs in the class assigned to v at i and w, t.

So, (the clause corresponding to) 'Felix is green' turns out to be true (i, w, t) iff Felix is among the things that are green in w, t; and (the clause corresponding to) 'I am green' turns out to be true (i, w, t) iff the agent of i belongs in the class for 'is green' with respect to w and t. In equivalent terms: solely on the basis of a clause's structure and of its components' contributions, the system assigns to a clause–index pair a t-distribution—that is, a mapping of points of evaluation to truth-values.

Since the structure of an index includes the kind of parameters relevant to a point—namely, a time and a world—the system's conclusions of t-distributions may eventually be interpreted as results of *unrelativized* truth-value (for clause–index pairs—or, equivalently, results of truth-value for a clause relativized only to an index). Informally, the idea behind this strategy is the commonsensical notion that, for instance, my utterance of 'Felix is on the mat', taking place on 1 December in front of Felix quietly sleeping on the rug, though false with respect to a variety of points, is true *simpliciter*, since it is true with respect to (the point corresponding to) the way things happen to be in the context of my utterance. Slightly more formally, a clause–index pair $<s, i>$ may be evaluated as True iff the system assigns to it the truth-value truth with respect to the point $<i_w, i_t>$, i.e., the point determined by the index. On the basis of this definition, the usual notions of logical properties and relations may then be defined in the customary manner. So, for instance, given certain traditional assumptions pertaining to 'if...then...', it may turn out that (the clause corresponding to) 'If Felix is on the mat, then Felix is on the mat' is True at all indexes; that 'Felix is on the mat and Felix is on the mat' is equivalent to 'Felix is on the mat', i.e., that for every index, the former is True iff the latter is; and, to cite a more interesting case, to be discussed in greater detail in

Chapter 2, that 'Felix is actually on the mat now if and only if Felix is on the mat' is logically valid.[12]

4. Representations

As I explained, interpretive systems take certain abstract items as input: namely, clause–index pairs. Systems may then be said to bear an interesting relationship to *utterances* on the basis of particular hypotheses pertaining to the clause-index appropriate in each case. In this manner, systems yield conditional assignments of t-distributions to utterances: on the assumption that a clause–index pair x is appropriate for an utterance y, the system assigns to y the t-distribution it assigns to x. In this case, I say that x is the pair appropriately *representing* y.

More often than not, the pair representing an utterance contains a clause suitably related to the uttered sentence and an index whose parameters correspond to certain appropriate aspects of that utterance. The nature of the 'suitable relation' holding between the clause in question and the uttered sentence involves difficult and important questions that are nevertheless of no immediate importance here. In fact, as I already indicated, in some of the examples in what follows I forget the distinction between sentences and clauses altogether, and I pretend that systems apply to constructs including an English sentence, rather than the more complex structures appropriate for more sophisticated semantic tasks. As for indexes, the correspondence between their parameters and the utterance under analysis is typically taken to be straightforward, at least in the case of the simple indexicals with which I am mainly concerned. Given an utterance u, so it is assumed, the agent of the appropriate

---

[12] For general discussions of validity within the 'Logic of Demonstratives', see e.g. Almog 1986; Crossley and Humberstone 1977; Kaplan 1977 and 1989; Lewis 1980.

index is the person who is producing (uttering, writing, etc.) u, the relevant time is the time when u takes place, and so on. I discuss this assumption and its significance in Chapter 2.

That systems operate only on the assumption of hypotheses of representation is, as far as I know, largely uncontroversial among the defenders of the traditional paradigm. What is by no means uncontroversial is the exact nature of the regularities to which the process of representation ought to pay attention. Take our discussion of a proposed law, with no birds in sight. Bored by our inconclusive exchange, I get absorbed by memories of my recent visit to the pet store. After you have finished your political tirade, I change the subject: I say 'That was an expensive bill', aimed at addressing the parrot's unreasonable price. If the prospective law was no worse than moderately expensive, and the pet store did indeed overcharge its customers, was my utterance true? That is, was representable by means of a clause–index pair which an adequate system would interpret as true? Did I say something true or something false by uttering the sentence I chose? Did the sentence I uttered, as uttered under those conditions, provide a true or a false description of how things actually were?[13]

None of these (possibly non-equivalent) queries regarding the aforementioned scenario seem answerable without a word of caution. There are fairly uncontroversial conclusions one may legitimately draw: for instance, on the one hand, that my utterance was likely not to achieve at least some of the intended communicative effects, and, on the other, that the sentence I uttered could sometimes be employed so as to convey that a certain beak is a costly item. I am unsure whether decisions pertaining to the most appropriate sense of 'what the speaker said' or 'what an utterance says' may by themselves lead to illuminating analyses of either of the conclusions I just

---

[13] For a discussion of related questions pertaining to the choice of so-called domain of discourse, see Gauker 1997a and 1998.

mentioned. Still, what rather uncontroversially must be the case is that decisions about the correct answers to the questions in the foregoing paragraph leave a variety of important questions open, including, in particular, the kind of issues systematically dealt with by systems of the type sketched in section 3. Suppose that, on the occasion of our not too smoothly co-ordinated conversation, my utterance *is* appropriately represented by means of an expression conventionally related to pieces of legislation—because, say, my wish to be addressing beaks is 'neutralized' by the absence of an explicit warning that I was about to change the subject, or by the fact that your expectations were geared towards a commentary on politics, rather than birds. This decision obviously does not exhaust the explanation of why, given the aforementioned hypothesis, my utterance ends up talking of the price of a proposed law. To the contrary, it is the system's responsibility that it maps the (representation of the) utterance in question to the intuitively appropriate results—say, an assignment of truth depending on the cost of the law, rather than one dependent upon the price of a bird, my favourite colour, or the height of the Empire State Building. Suppose, on the other hand, that my intentions do matter and that, regardless of the problems you may have in decoding it, the appropriate representation of my utterance includes an expression conventionally related to beaks. It is, once again, the system's task to unveil the systematic mechanisms in virtue of which the clause–index pair thus selected ends up with the desired t-distribution, rather than, say, with an account in which it turns out to be entailed by 'That was an inexpensive beak'.[14]

To summarize: the system proceeds on the basis of certain claims pertaining to the conventional meaning of particular

---

[14] A distinct but parallel issue has to do with the choice of the *demonstratum* parameter within the appropriate index and the role played in this respect by intentions and demonstrations. On this see in particular Bach 1992; Reimer 1991*a* and 1991*b*; Kaplan 1977 and 1989.

items, suitably related to English expressions. Given these hypotheses, the system reaches results of t-distributions with respect to indexes and, eventually, conclusions pertaining to the logical relationships between the constructs under examination. These results may be applied eventually to particular utterances, given other independent assumptions. These assumptions pertain to the type of construct appropriate for the case under analysis, and to the parameters needed for the evaluation of those expressions which, in virtue of their character, interestingly appeal to appropriate *relata* for their evaluation. That our intuitions about particular instances may be confronted with the system's result only on the basis of independent hypotheses of representation does not of course entail that any outcome of t-distributions may be understood appropriately as intuitively adequate, provided that representational hypotheses are ingeniously tampered with. To the contrary, the interpretive system's adequacy *vis-à-vis* particular intuitions of truth-value remains directly assessable, albeit in a conditional fashion: if your utterance of 'This is an expensive bill' is to be interpreted, for one reason or another, as directed toward beaks rather than laws, systems applied to an appropriate input ought to render truth-values dependent upon the cost of a bird, regardless of the fact of the matter in political economy. By the same token, the system's outcome remains immediately responsible with respect to particular intuitions of logical relations. Given the only relevant sense in which utterances of 'Either this is an expensive bill or this is not an expensive bill' may be said to be warrantedly true (in a sense which will be discussed throughout this essay), the system's treatment of 'not' and 'either...or' must be such that, given the relevant clause, a result of validity is forthcoming. That some utterances of 'Either this is an expensive bill or this is not an expensive bill' may turn out false, because different items are denoted by the demonstratives or because different senses of 'bill' are at issue, is obviously not worrisome for a result of this kind.

It is undeniable that traditional systems, understood along these lines, leave unaddressed many issues that are of immediate relevance for a hearer interested in interpreting and evaluating her interlocutor's speech. For instance, traditional systems are unable to determine the resolution of ambiguities or the unpacking of ellipses, just as they are, unsurprisingly, inefficient at making a good cup of coffee or resolving domestic disputes. However, they are, or at least appear to be, surprisingly efficient when it comes to the task for which they are developed—and, in particular, quite informative when it comes to a variety of aspects of the relationships between meaning, truth, and the use of language. Precisely in so far as they put forth a certain approach to these fundamental concepts, traditional systems have raised a not inconsiderable degree of controversy: the view of meaning and truth they embed, so it is occasionally objected, is inadequate. I return to the main argumentative line against customary systems in Chapter 4, after the discussion of certain misunderstandings for which even the foremost defenders of the traditional paradigm are responsible. Some preliminary considerations are, however, appropriate already at this stage: sections 5 and 6 are devoted to a brief discussion of questions of representation, disambiguation, and reference assignment *vis-à-vis* a fashionable sceptical attitude towards customary semantic standpoints.

5. *Disambiguation and Reference Assignment*

A characteristic theme in the ordinary language tradition from the Fifties had to do with the relationships between the semantic behaviour of the logical constants in simple formal languages, such as the standard language for propositional logic, and the interpretation of certain everyday locutions. This issue was particularly prominent in Strawson's *Introduction to Logical Theory*

(1952), a work later reviewed by Quine in 'Mr Strawson on Logical Theory' (Quine 1953). Strawson's point, incidentally, had very little to do with the contemporary form of semantic scepticism I shall discuss in Chapter 4. His views regarding 'and', for instance, seem eminently plausible. It goes without saying that, regardless of whether I am right in my sympathy with Strawson on this issue, nothing inherently damaging for the framework of natural language semantics is likely to follow. Quine, who was addressing Strawson's more general concerns about logical theory, unhesitatingly declares his admiration for Strawson's sensitivity to 'the speech of natural man'.

> Logic... is *formal* logic in a narrow sense which excludes those preparatory operations, in applied logic, whereby sentences of ordinary language are fitted to logical forms by interpretation and paraphrase. Mr. Strawson stresses the magnitude of these applicational manœuvres, and in this I am in full agreement. (Quine 1953: 142)

Even though the issue on the table in the Quine–Strawson debate does not pertain to the scope and limits of the contemporary semantics' research programme, Quine's methodological point with respect to 'interpretation and paraphrase' is also of relevance with respect to the issue pertaining to the 'preparatory operations' required for the application of the system's interpretive structure. The issue now is not (or at least need not be) one surrounding the appropriate paraphrase of the vernacular into the formulas of, say, first-order logic with identity. Still, Quine's assessment of the magnitude of the required 'applicational manœuvres', and of its relationship to the inner workings of semantic interpretation, is also illuminating for the topic of this essay. He writes:

> Insofar as the interpretation of ambiguous expressions depends on circumstances of the argument as a whole—speaker, hearer, scene, date, and underlying problem and purpose—the fallacy of equivocation is not to be feared; for, those background circumstances may be

expected to influence the interpretation of an ambiguous expression uniformly wherever the expression recurs in the course of the argument. (Quine 1953: 146)

The system's analysis of meaning and truth entails results regarding logical properties and relations—validity, entailment, equivalence, etc. Results such as these and, more generally, conclusions of t-distributions may be applied to particular examples only on the basis of given hypotheses of representation. Still, adapting Quine's point to the present topic, the system's logical outcome may be assessed for unconditional adequacy in a straightforward manner, as long as the relevant 'background circumstances' (that is, the motivations for one representational choice or another) are kept constant across the relevant variables.

Nevertheless, questions pertaining to, among other things, resolution of ambiguity, unpacking of ellipsis, or assignment of reference are occasionally cited as revealing intrinsic weaknesses in one or another approach to semantics. The target is, more often than not, Grice's theory of conversational implicatures, according to which maxims such as Relevance operate on the basis of the literal message encoded within an utterance. Since it seems plausible to suppose that at least some of the maxims play a role in interpretive processes determinant for the literal 'what is said', what results is a presumably troublesome predicament:

[Grice] draws a major distinction between what is actually said and what is tacitly implicated, suggesting that every aspect of interpretation can be assigned to one or another category.... It seems to follow, within Grice's framework, that (a) the maxims play no role in determining what is said, and (b) any aspect of interpretation governed by the maxims must be analysable as a conversational implicature. In fact, neither of these claims seems to be true. (Wilson and Sperber 1981: 156)

This may well raise interesting scholarly issues regarding the correct interpretation of Grice's own take on conversational implicature—even though I did not manage to find, in the letter of Grice's work, unequivocal indications favouring (a) and (b).[15] Equally doubtful, in the absence of arguments to the contrary, is that (a) and (b) 'follow' from Grice's more general premises, or that they are essentially part and parcel of his wider approach. But it is not Grice's approach to implicatures and 'what is said' that is important for my project here, but the significance of the positive conclusion which Sperber, Wilson, and others put forth in this respect: namely, that 'the disambiguation of utterances, and the assignment of reference to their referring phrases, must fall squarely within the domain of pragmatics' (Wilson and Sperber 1981: 157–8). Presumably, 'pragmatics' is here supposed to cover processes that are not (or at least not solely) guided by the conventional meaning of the expressions under analysis, and that involve reasoning patterns highly sensitive to contextual factors such as, to use Quine's locution, 'speaker, hearer, scene, date, and underlying problem and purpose'. In this sense, unquestionably and rather obviously, disambiguation and reference assignment are pragmatic businesses. Still nothing, in the absence of further arguments, follows from this commonsensical tenet that is of relevance for the assessment of the structures that I have presented thus far. Yet, without further ado, the polemical focus quickly, albeit only temporarily, shifts away from Grice: 'The point is often overlooked: cf. Kaplan ["Dthat"], Stalnaker ["Pragmatics"], who suggest that context alone can determine disambiguation' (Wilson and Sperber 1981: n. 4). Focusing on the source of most immediate relevance for my topic, I must confess that, after repeated readings of 'Dthat' and Kaplan's other essays on indexicals, I remain unable to identify any commitment to a particular view of disambiguation, let alone to anything that may be summarized as the thesis that 'context alone can determine disambiguation', in any informative sense of the phrase. The fuzzy notion that 'context alone' may do the job is once again

---

[15] See Neale 1992: 530 and the discussion in Carston 2002: 105.

attributed to Kaplan in Anne Bezuidenhout's paper on the referential/attributive distinction, an essay squarely in syntony with Sperber and Wilson's sceptical stance. Focusing this time on reference assignment, rather than disambiguation, Bezuidenhout writes:

The idea that the representation of the LF of an utterance may not yield a complete proposition has long been recognised, though it was generally assumed that disambiguation and reference assignment were the only things needed to yield a complete proposition. Moreover, reference assignment was frequently supposed simply to be a matter of searching the context for an object which satisfied the descriptive character associated with the expression. This is the way that Kaplan, for example, conceives of reference assignment for the class of expressions he calls pure indexicals (see Kaplan [Demonstratives], p. 491). (Bezuidenhout 1997: 387)

And, in more general terms, Stephen Levinson, during a short break from his sustained attack on certain aspects of Grice's approach, once again targets the traditional approach to semantics for its presumed insistence that natural language sentences be directly interpreted on the basis of the system's regularities.

There is no algorithm that, given a syntactic string in a language, cranks out its unique logical form or semantic structure. The view that there *is* such an algorithm forms the basis of much linguistic theorising from Montague to Chomsky's most recent views. But it is patently absurd to hold such a view. First, there is the enormous range of ambiguities in natural language (requiring at least a one-to-many correspondence). (Levinson 2000: 8)

It must surely be at first arresting to be told that figures of the calibre of Chomsky and Montague, and with views on semantics as dramatically different as those of Chomsky and Montague, manage to find a point of agreement in what is in fact a 'patently absurd' tenet. The effect of surprise does not last for long—no longer, indeed, than it takes for a cursory examination of 'much linguistic theorising from Montague to Chomsky'. For undoubtedly, traditional semantic structures, such as the system I presented in section 1, do not at all provide a decision pertaining to the appropriate disambiguation of a natural language sentence or a definite conclusion regarding the contextual items appropriate for the interpretation of an indexical expression. They do, on the other hand, present precise conclusions pertaining to certain properties of a given utterance, on the basis of independently established hypotheses pertaining to the clause-index suitably representing it. As an immediate consequence, and as already perspicuously indicated in the passage from Quine cited above, they provide definite results pertaining to the relationships between certain items, on the assumption that whatever parameters may affect their interpretations are assumed to be fixed throughout the process.

I am perplexed by Sperber and Wilson's reading of Kaplan. Bezuidenhout's error, on the other hand, is worthy of further discussion, possibly being grounded in a terminological confusion to which I already alluded above when I chose to label the collection of parameters invoked by the indexicals' characters as 'index', rather than, as Kaplan, Lewis, and many others do, 'context'. There is an obvious sense in which, in Kaplan's approach, the reference of an indexical is determined by 'searching the context for an object which satisfied the descriptive character' of that expression: what is being 'searched' is, rather trivially, the type of parameter which, according to the expression's character, needs to be searched—in the terminology introduced above, the co-ordinate within the *index* that the indexical's meaning prescribes as important for its interpretation. Still, even though indexes are labelled by Kaplan as 'contexts', it seems obvious that Kaplan's austere n-tuples are not 'contexts' in the everyday sense of the word—that is, in the sense of the word eventually responsible for the evaluation of particular instances involving the use of an indexical. When it comes to indexicals and context, in this latter sense of the term, their relationship is not, or at least need not be, any more immediate and formally encoded in the traditional approach than Bezuidenhout (and common sense) may desire. What an indexical's 'descriptive character' targets, in a straightforward fashion, are parameters within the index, such as 'the agent' or 'the *demonstratum*'. What is by no means straightforward, given a particular situation in which speaking occurs, is who the agent or the *demonstratum* are.

As indicated by Levinson's 'First', in the sentence concluding the passage I quoted above, other, and potentially more serious, problems are supposed to affect the traditional approach to semantics. It is for this reason that the versions of anti-traditional scepticism put forth by Levinson, Sperber, Bezuidenhout, Wilson, and others are by no means neutralized by my considerations in this section. A more thorough discussion of their arguments will have to wait until Chapter 4, where I directly confront the challenge presented by the so-called contextualist standpoint. As for questions of disambiguation, reference assignment, and the like, it should be pointed out that at least some of the champions of the contextualist cause recognize that other aspects of the traditional paradigm are presumably more fertile targets for their attacks. Robyn Carston, for instance, takes a clear stand in favour of the contextualist side when it comes to issues of truth-conditions, full articulation, and free enrichment, but is quite clear that, when it comes to ambiguity, the pragmatist's concerns, though clearly distinct from those of natural language semanticists, may peacefully coexist with them.

The way ambiguity... is reflected in truth-conditional theories highlights the difference between this sort of semantic theory and the cognitive processing account of utterance understanding that I am working towards. A semantics for an n-ways ambiguous natural language string is complete once it has provided n different T(ruth)-sentences in the metalanguage... This is obviously not a trivial undertaking, but the point is that the n different sentences are distinguished in advance of their treatment by the truth theory. What the pragmatic theory must confront is the very different issue of how the hearer recognizes... the one... of these *n* possibilities. (Carston 2002: 21)

6. Tradition and Indexes

In all likelihood, the structures I hypothesized as candidates for an index are lacking in some important respect: a list including only an agent, a time, a location, a possible world, and a *demonstratum* must surely leave some English indexicals unsatisfied in the kind of search which their characters impose upon them. Worse than that, some issues pertaining to the sufficiency of my impoverished indexes unquestionably need to be addressed also with respect to the very few indexicals with which I am concerned: in particular with the demonstrative 'that'. For instance, in my simple-minded sketch, indexes contain one unique individual as a *demonstratum*. Still, utterances of sentences containing multiple occurrences of 'that', such as 'That is taller than that', may intuitively be interpretable as addressing two distinct items. If it is taken for granted that the representation for an utterance such as this involves one unique index, it follows that at least one of the occurrences of 'that' ends up with the wrong referent.

The undeniable differences between, say, the demonstrative 'that' and the non-demonstrative 'I' may or may not force a choice between interestingly different technical options.[16] But it is not the relationship between demonstratives and demonstrations, and the related problem of multiple occurrences of a demonstrative, that concern me here, but rather the discussion of an alleged fundamental distinction between demonstratives and non-demonstrative indexicals more directly relevant for my

---

[16] For a discussion of related issues, see Caplan 2003.

discussion of representational issues. The presumed distinction I have in my mind is occasionally discussed with a polemic, anti-traditionalist intent, but never with such explicitness as in François Recanati's work on 'saturation'.

Non-demonstrative indexicals, Recanati points out, are relatively unexciting: everybody and his dog know that 'I' depends on context. It does so, Recanati adds, in a straightforward manner. In the case of 'I',

> the contextual assignment is automatic and rule-governed. Thus the reference of 'I' is determined automatically on the basis of a linguistic rule, without taking the speaker's beliefs and intentions into consideration. (Recanati 2002a: 299)

Allegedly of greater interest are other, presumably more pragmatically oriented instances of indexicality. Indeed, their alleged significance is such that, in Recanati's discussion of the reasons why 'there is something deeply wrong with the standard picture', these indexicals appear at the top of the list (2001: 85). A recurrent example is provided by instances involving genitive constructions such as 'John's car', which Recanati interprets in terms of an expression containing a free relation-variable, roughly along the lines of 'the car that bears relation R to John'. As indicated by the passages I quote later in this section, demonstratives such as 'that' also fall within what Recanati takes to be the more exciting instances of 'saturation'—that is, those expressions that demand contextual contributions by virtue of their character, but whose relationships with context are less 'automatic' than that at issue with 'I'. Recanati writes:

> The free variable must be contextually assigned a particular value; but that value is not determined by a rule and is not a function of a particular aspect of the narrow context. What a given occurrence of the phrase 'John's car' means ultimately depends upon what the speaker who utters it means. (Recanati 2001: 85; see also Recanati 2002a: 299)

Given the very wide array of possible interpretations of the variable in question (the car John owns, the car he drives, the car on which he bet, the car in which he is sitting...), the contextual dependence affecting possessive constructions seems to Recanati to be of a fundamentally different type than that relevant to 'pure indexicals':

> the type of context-dependence exhibited by (pure) indexicals has nothing to do with the radical form of context-dependence which affects speaker's meaning. The hallmark of the more radical form of context-dependence is the fact that any piece of contextual information may be relevant. But the context that comes into play in the semantic interpretation of [pure] indexicals is... a very limited context which contains only a few aspects of the pragmatic context: who speaks, when, where, and so forth. (Recanati 2001: 85)[17]

I am perplexed with respect to the relevance of Recanati's distinction. What exactly is at issue? One difference is undeniable: namely, that in a variety of typical instances involving the use of 'I' one may easily determine who the referent is: if it is granted that the contextually salient agent is the speaker, establishment of reference is 'automatic', *as long as* one knows who the speaker is. When it comes to the interpretation of possessive constructions (or demonstratives), the process may well be less straightforward: pragmatic questions of salience, and in particular the discussion of the speaker's communicative intentions, undoubtedly play a role. Yet, leaving such practical differences aside, it is equally the case that, *as long as* one knows what the salient relation (or *demonstratum*) is, semantic interpretation is as 'automatic' here as for 'I' or 'now'. Representational questions may well be easier, and less dependent upon speaker meaning, for 'I' and 'now' than for other instances of the genitive or for demonstratives (though

---

[17] The relationship addressed by the genitive (say, the relationship between John and a certain car) may in fact be more strongly constrained than these comments may indicate; see Storto 2002.

even this weaker claim should appear dubious by the end of Chapter 2). But why should such a presumed difference be problematic for the traditional approach?

Demonstratives provide fairly explicit evidence for my suspicion that the presumed 'radical form of context dependence' assessed by Recanati is by no means incompatible with the customary view. For instance, in that epitome of traditionalism that is Kaplan 1977, questions pertaining to the profile of a *demonstrative* within the system responsible for compositional analysis are firmly distinguished from the issue of the structure and role of a *demonstration*—so much so that Kaplan, one of the most outspoken critics of a Fregean theory of singular terms, sympathetically (even if only temporarily) entertains a Fregean theory of demonstrations. Yet, Recanati writes, when it comes to demonstratives, traditionalists

> will add to the narrow context a sequence of 'speaker's intended referents', in such a way that the *n*th demonstrative in the sentence will refer to the *n*th member of the sequence. Formally that is fine, but philosophically it is clear that one is cheating. We pretend that we can manage with a limited, narrow notion of context of the sort we need for handling indexicals, while in fact we can only determine the speaker's intended referent... by resorting to pragmatic interpretation and relying on the *wide* context. (Recanati 2001: 86)

Leaving aside the questions possibly raised by multiple occurrences of demonstratives, and focusing on the idea that a demonstrative's character addresses a *demonstratum* co-ordinate in the index, it is unclear what Recanati's distinction between fine formalism and philosophical cheating amounts to. What is intelligible is another distinction, that between the function for indexes within traditional interpretive systems, and the role that 'wide context' ought to play in determining the appropriate index within the representation for an utterance. There is no reason to believe that an adequate analysis of the latter turns out to be incompatible with anyone's account of demonstratives, *a fortiori* with the traditional approach to their semantic contribution.

Far from pointing to a form of pragmatic intrusion incompatible with the traditional paradigm, the aforementioned distinction between 'pure indexicals' and demonstratives does in fact belittle the scope of such intrusions. As I argue in the next chapter, it is by no means the case that expressions such as 'I' derive their referent in an 'automatic' fashion, independently of the speaker's intentions or of other, presumably 'pragmatic' factors. As I explained, a conclusion of this kind, regardless of whether it is directed to 'I' or to 'that', is not problematic for the paradigm I described in this chapter. Still, questions of significance from the interpretive system's point of view will emerge, pertaining to the structure of an index and, consequently, to the system's assessment of logical validity. Interestingly, so I shall argue, important misunderstandings of these issues characterize not only the sceptical attitude which I began to discuss in this and the previous sections, but also the positions defended by some foremost exponents of the traditional paradigm.

7. *Where Am I Now?*

In this chapter I have explained that interpretive systems operate on abstract items of a particular type, clause–index pairs, and yield results of t-distributions. Clauses and indexes bear an interesting relationship to some of the semantically important aspects of an utterance: respectively the uttered expressions and some relevant contextual parameters. On the basis of hypotheses pertaining to such a relationship, systems may then be interpreted as assigning t-distributions to utterances, and may be evaluated for empirical adequacy on the basis of our intuitions about them. In the next chapters, I focus on some controversial aspects of the relationship between systems and utterances. In Chapter 2,

I discuss the interface between contexts and indexes, and I analyse the system's commitments to certain results of validity with respect to indexical languages. In Chapter 3, I motivate the system's indirect approach to utterances, and I criticize the proposals put forth by the so-called token-reflexivity movement. In Chapter 4, I return to the anti-traditionalist theme that I touched on only preliminarily in the final sections of this chapter.

Chapter 2
Systems and Indexes

As explained in Chapter 1, traditional interpretive systems relativize the evaluation of indexical expressions to indexes. This relativization is intended to reflect within the system's structure an obvious and intuitive feature of those expressions: in virtue of their meaning, words such as 'I' or 'now' pick up a given individual or time only with respect to certain features of what is commonly called a 'context'. Still, the system's proposal that 'I' or 'now' be associated with non-constant characters yields results comparable with our intuitions only on the assumption that indexes bear a suitable relation to the sort of items we intuitively understand as determining the semantic profile of such expressions on given occasions. In the terminology of Chapter 1, the system's results may be applied to an utterance only on the basis of correct hypotheses pertaining to the representation of (among other things) the relevant contextual background in the austere format of a collection of co-ordinates.

Hypotheses of this type, dealing with the index suitable for the representation of an utterance, have not received an amount of attention comparable to that devoted to the representation of the uttered expressions. Perhaps this dismissive attitude is grounded in the assumption that the solution to this question is straightforward. Here, in particular, is a simple picture that does indeed often yield the correct outcome. Suppose that, on 20 June, I say

(1) I am bored today.

It is relatively unproblematic to extract an index appropriate to the situation in which my utterance has taken place. In this example, it contains myself as the agent, and 20 June as the temporal co-ordinate. Pair this index and the sentence-type (1), or whatever syntactic representation you deem appropriate, and take into consideration the characters for 'I' and 'today'. What you reach, on the basis of any straightforward interpretive system, is the (correct) conclusion that my utterance says of myself and of 20 June that the former is bored on the latter, i.e., that my utterance is true just in case I was bored on that day. This point of view may easily be adapted to instances involving written messages. Suppose for instance that, on 15 March, in Los Angeles, I write 'Now the trees are blooming here' in a letter to a friend. My inscription occurs in a context apparently corresponding to an index that contains 15 March and Los Angeles as, respectively, its temporal and spatial parameters. If one applies the customary characters of 'here' and 'now' to such an index, one obtains the (correct) results that my letter says that the trees are blooming in Los Angeles on 15 March and that my inscription is true iff that is indeed the case.[1]

The procedure sketched thus far is often implicitly assumed to be generalizable to all sorts of examples. I label as the *Simple-Minded View* the claim that utterances (or inscriptions) are always correctly represented by means of indexes whose co-ordinates correspond in an obvious manner to the parameters of the context

[1] 'Now' may refer to temporal intervals that properly include the temporal parameter of the index. Analogous considerations hold, *mutatis mutandis*, for 'here'. Thus, the sentence in my letter may be used to convey the information that, say, the trees are blooming in Southern California in early spring. This complication, however, is not directly relevant to the topic of this essay, and I shall ignore it in what follows.

of utterance (or inscription). More precisely: given an utterance *u*, I refer to the index including the speaker and the time, location, and world at which the utterance takes place, as the *simple-minded* index for *u* (similarly, *mutatis mutandis*, for inscriptions). According to the Simple-Minded View, an utterance or inscription *u* of a sentence *S* is true iff the pair consisting of (the clause appropriate for) *S* and of the simple-minded index for *u* is assigned the truth-value Truth by an appropriate interpretive system.

The Simple-Minded View is the principal target of the first half of this chapter. Against it, I present a variety of examples that cannot be handled correctly by evaluating the expressions at issue with respect to the simple-minded index. I begin with cases involving written notes and recording devices, and I criticize analyses that strive to remain consistent with the Simple-Minded View. I then explain why my take on recorded messages may also be applied profitably to a variety of other cases.

Yet, this essay's main aim does not pertain directly to the 'preparatory operations' eventually yielding an input appropriate from the system's point of view. What is more immediately important are the assumptions regarding truth and meaning that traditional systems presuppose, and their relationship to particular instances involving the use of language. My attack on the Simple-Minded View in the first sections of this chapter is of relevance not merely as an analysis of certain relatively peripheral phenomena, such as written notes or the historical present, but especially as a pedagogical introduction to questions having to do with the outcomes on truth, meaning, and logic to which the traditional approach is committed. In section 4, I focus on Kaplan's approach to indexical languages, and on certain peculiar truths of the logic of indexicals. I return to another application of my views on indexes in the final section, where I address some issues related to fictional discourse.

As section 4 reveals, and as will be confirmed in later chapters, my description of the interpretive systems of Chapter 1 as 'traditional' is not commemorative. What is important from my point of view is a defence of the approach to meaning and truth inevitably entangled in structures of that type, possibly regardless of the contrary views put forth by the traditional defenders, or even the founding fathers, of the paradigm I wish to analyse. Indeed, it is my contention in what follows that customary systems have been at least partially misunderstood not only by 'outsiders' such as the contextualist pragmatists whom I shall confront in Chapter 4, but also by semanticists working squarely within the established approach to natural languages.

1. *Written and Recorded Messages*

Take the story of Jones, who suddenly decides to flee the country. Before leaving home at eight in the morning, he writes a note to his wife, who will be back from work at five in the evening:

(2) As you can see, I am not at home now. If you hurry, you'll catch the evening flight to Los Cabos. Meet me in six hours at the Hotel Cabo Real.

Clearly, the note does not intuitively convey the false message that Jones is not at home at the time the note was written, nor does it request that Mrs Jones be at the Cabo Real at two in the afternoon, i.e., six hours from the time of inscription. And suppose that you write in your office

(3) I am here now

on a scrap of paper, and that, after having arrived home, you leave it on the kitchen table, with the intention of informing someone of your whereabouts. Your note does not say (falsely) that you are at the location of inscription, i.e., in your office; it rather conveys the (correct) information that you are in the house.

The intuitively correct interpretation of these examples may easily be obtained, on the basis of the obvious characters for 'I', 'here', and 'now', and of straightforward assumptions pertaining to the interpretive system's structure, if the index taken into consideration by the system contains co-ordinates intended by the speaker as semantically relevant, even if distinct from the obvious items within the context of utterance/inscription—that is, if the index the system considers is different from the simple-minded index.[2] In the case of (2), the index yielding the appropriate outcome contains as its temporal co-ordinate the expected time of Mrs Jones's arrival, five o'clock in the afternoon, rather than the time at which Jones wrote the note, eight in the morning. With respect to this index, 'now' and 'in six hours' succeed in picking up 5 p.m. and 11 p.m. according to their customary characters. Analogously, in the case of (3), the appropriate index contains your house as its spatial parameter, and not the place where you wrote the note. Since 'here' refers to the index's spatial parameter, your inscription may then be interpreted in the intuitively correct manner, i.e., as imparting the information that you are in your house.

That the Simple-Minded View must be on the wrong track is concisely brought to light by cases involving the negation of (3): that is, by apparently true instances of

(4) I am not here now.

As sanctioned by the straightforward interpretive system sketched in Chapter 1,

---

[2] The suggestion that the appropriate index contains the co-ordinates *intended* as relevant by the speaker is controversial—see in particular Corazza *et al.* 2002; Gorvett, forthcoming; Romdenh-Romluc 2002; and my reply in Predelli 2002*b*. But the issue is not of immediate relevance to the aim of this chapter, the rejection of the Simple-Minded View: although we disagree on the criteria for the identification of the relevant index, my critics and I agree that it may well be distinct from the simple-minded index. On these issues, see also Perry 2003.

(a) the characters of the English expressions 'I', 'here', and 'now' are such that the referents of these expressions with respect to an index i are, respectively, the agent, the location, and the time of i.

But according to the Simple-Minded View,

(b) an utterance or inscription u is appropriately represented by means of the pair $<s, i>$, where s is the clause suitable for u and i is the simple-minded index for u.

It follows from (a) and (b) that utterances of 'I', 'here', and 'now' refer, respectively, to the utterer, the location of utterance, and the time of utterance (or, in the case of inscriptions, to the writer, the location of inscription, and the time of inscription). So, together with some other uncontroversial premisses, it follows that 'I am here now' is uttered truly iff the utterer is at the location of utterance at the time of utterance (similarly for the case of inscription). However, it may seem that

(c) an utterer is at the location of utterance at the time of utterance (or inscription).

It follows from the Simple-Minded View, together with the aforementioned premisses, that 'I am not here now' may never be uttered/written truly. But this result clashes with our intuition that there are true instances of 'I am not here now', written on a scrap of paper or reproduced by a recording device. An analogous difficulty is raised by utterances of 'I exist (now)'. Given the thesis that 'I' and 'now' refer to the utterer and the time of utterance, together with

(d) a speaker exists at the time of utterance (or inscription),

it follows that 'I exist (now)' may not be uttered or written falsely. But this conclusion is also at odds with our intuitions concerning certain instances of written notes and recorded

Systems and Indexes ~ 45

messages. For instance, 'I do not exist any longer' may well occur truly as part of one's will.[3]

Although the foregoing analysis of (2) and (3), and the corresponding diagnosis of the problem with the Simple-Minded treatment of (4) seem to me to have a great deal of initial plausibility, they are by no means the standard accounts of recorded and written messages. In the next section, I briefly discuss some alternative views on this subject.

2. Multiple Characters and Remote Utterances

According to some, examples similar to those discussed above indicate that indexical expressions are ambiguous, and that they are sometimes associated with a character that does not yield the obvious parameter of the relevant index. We find a premonition of such a *Many Characters View* in a suggestion that David Kaplan attributes to Keith Donnellan in a footnote to 'Demonstratives'. According to it, 'our language might contain two forms of "now": one for the time of production, another for the time of audition' (Kaplan 1977: 491 n. 12).[4] Some years later, a similar view is endorsed by Quentin Smith (1989). Among other examples, Smith discusses an utterance of 'Today is January 27', recorded on 26 January and broadcast the following day. He comments:

[The customary character of 'today'] is inapplicable [in this case] and instead another rule is applicable, viz., that 'today' takes us to the day *the reproductions of the utterance are heard by the audience*. (Smith 1989: 172)

---

[3] This example occurs in Salmon 1991: 176 n. 21.

[4] But Donnellan presents this view only as a description of a possible language, one which could be operative 'if there were typically a significant lag between our production of speech and its audition (for example, if sound travelled very very slowly)' (Kaplan 1977: 491 n. 12).

These suggestions may be developed in the following manner. Let indexes include (at least) two temporal co-ordinates, corresponding to the time when the utterance is produced and the time when it is received by the audience. Label these co-ordinates as, respectively, the *encoding time* and the *decoding time*.[5] According to the Many Characters View, temporal indexicals are ambiguously anchored to either temporal co-ordinate, and the appropriate level of lexical representation ought to distinguish between, say, 'today$_{ET}$', associated by a satisfactory interpretive system with the day containing the encoding time, and 'today$_{DT}$', mapped to the time of decoding (similarly, of course, for 'now' and other temporal indexicals). Jones's note (2) is then allegedly represented by means of a clause roughly along the lines of

(2′) ...I am not at home now$_{DT}$.... Meet me [in six hours]$_{DT}$ at the Hotel Cabo Real,

where [in six hours]$_{DT}$ is understood as 'in six hours from now$_{DT}$'. If the Many Characters View is applied to spatial indexicals in an obvious way, it also seems to entail the intuitively correct reading of your note, as long as it is disambiguated as

(3′) I am here$_{DL}$,

where here$_{DL}$ is interpreted as referring to the location of decoding. The rejection of premiss (a) entailed by the Many Characters View also suggests a straightforward solution to the puzzle of apparently true utterances of (4): depending on the meaning with which they are used, the indexicals in question may end up picking up an individual *a*, location *l*, and time *t*, such that *a* may well fail to be in *l* and *t*.

In a slightly different version of the suggestion under analysis, proposed by Julia Colterjohn and Duncan MacIntosh (1987), the type of ambiguity at issue lies in the apparent fact that 'here'

---

[5] This terminology is borrowed from Fillmore 1975.

admits of a demonstrative use. When used along these lines, 'here' may pick up a location distinct from where the speaker happens to be—in the case of (3), the location where the note is being left. As they write, in this case 'the note is a "proxy-finger", which can be used to refer to wherever it itself is' (Colterjohn and MacIntosh 1987: 59–60). The demonstrative use of 'here' also unproblematically allows for true instances of (4): indicating a section of a map of Los Angeles, I may say 'I am not here now', thereby conveying the true information that I am not in Southern California at the time of utterance.

Notwithstanding its success with the few examples presented thus far, the Many Characters View leaves me unconvinced. The version proposed by Colterjohn and MacIntosh, in particular, suffers from a special defect, due to its insistence on a certain account of the demonstration allegedly attached to 'here'. In their view 'here' operates as a demonstrative accompanied by a 'proxy finger' pointing to wherever the note itself is. But it is not the case that 'here' inevitably ends up referring to the place where the note happens to end up. Suppose that I write 'I am not here' on a scrap of paper, and that I attach it to my door. Imagine also that, due to unforeseen and unintended circumstances, my note ends up in your living-room. I take it to be sufficiently uncontroversial that 'here' in my note does *not* refer to 'wherever the note itself is', i.e., to your living-room.

Moreover, and more importantly, no suggestion which focuses solely on the semantics of 'here' suffices as a solution to the analogous problem generated by utterances that do not involve any occurrence of 'here', such as the puzzle of true instances of 'I do not exist now' in a will. In this respect, the version of the Many Characters View presented at the beginning of this section may initially seem to be in a more promising position: what it suggests is the assignment of a multitude of characters not only to 'here', but also to 'today', 'now', and presumably 'I'. But such an improbable multiplication of characters is in fact *not* an advantage over the limited scope of Colterjohn and MacIntosh's suggestion. To the contrary, positions such as Quentin Smith's bring to light the inevitable fact that, if the right results are to be reached in a variety of distinct instances, each indexical ought to be associated within the interpretive system with a variety of unrelated characters, assigned to it by virtue of the conventions regulating its semantic behaviour. Thus, for instance, it would have to be a brute fact about the meaning(s) of 'today' that it sometimes refers to the time of utterance, at other times manages to pick out the day of reproduction, and in other circumstances, such as some of the examples I present below, denotes an interval intended as relevant by the speaker. Smith aims at masking the arbitrary aspect of such a collection by assuming that the various characters are collected under a unique semantic rule, which he refers to as a 'metacharacter'. Still, in any version of the Many Characters View, the ability of 'today' to refer to periods different from the day of utterance would have to be antecedently encoded, once and for all, in the meaning arbitrarily associated with that expression (similarly for 'now', 'I', 'here', and other indexicals). But it seems incredible that, merely by virtue of, say, the emergence of reproductive devices, 'today' undergoes a change of meaning, in order to enrich its metacharacter with the indication of the ability to pick out the time of reproduction.

The Many Characters View is not the only alternative to the denial of the Simple-Minded View. According to what I call the *Remote Utterance View*, defended by Alan Sidelle (1991), written notes and tape-recorders are contraptions that allow a speaker to perform utterances 'at a distance'; i.e., they are devices that make it possible for someone to utter a sentence at a time t and location l without actually being in l at t. Given the possibility of remote utterances, so this view continues, it is not implausible to conclude that Jones 'uttered' (2) at five o'clock, when Mrs Jones read the note, and that you 'uttered' (3) in your house, where your message was decoded by your addressee. If this is correct, then the desired results may be obtained with respect to the co-ordinates sanctioned by the Simple-Minded View, without concocting special characters for the indexicals in question, and, more generally, without deviating from the simple interpretive system of Chapter 1. In other words, as prescribed by the Simple-Minded View, the utterances/inscriptions under discussion are appropriately representable by means of the simple-minded index—that is, the index containing the time and location of utterance.

As for the puzzle of true instances of (4), Sidelle begins his reasoning against premiss (c) with the claim that 'I', 'here', and 'now' in a typical recorded or written message refer, respectively, to the encoder, the decoding location, and the decoding time. For instance, 'I', 'here', and 'now' occurring in my answering machine's message 'I am not here now' refer to myself, my house, and the time of the call. But it follows from (a) and (b) that 'here' and 'now' refer to the location and the time of utterance. Thus, the decoding location and the decoding time must be the location and the time of an utterance, hence 'there is an utterance at [decoding time]' (Sidelle 1991: 533). It also follows from (a) and (b) that 'I' in the message refers to the utterer, and hence that the encoder is the utterer. Given that the encoder is not at the decoding location at decoding time, 'it follows that a person need not be in the location of his utterance at the time of that utterance' (Sidelle 1991: 533), in contrast with the claim in (c). This reasoning may easily be adapted to true instances of 'I do not exist (now)'. The result in this latter case entails the negation of (d), i.e., the rejection of the thesis that the utterer always exists at the time of utterance.

In Sidelle's view, when one writes a note or records a message, one is merely 'arranging to make an utterance at a later time, or, if one likes, *deferring* an utterance', and '[t]he genuine utterance(s) will occur when someone calls and hears the message'

(Sidelle 1991: 535). The parameters relevant for the evaluation of a recorded message, Sidelle argues, are those in the context of *genuine utterance*, rather than the co-ordinates of the context in which encoding takes place. Thus, once the true context of utterance is identified, the appropriate representations of the example under analysis need involve no index other than the simple-minded index: namely, the index containing utterer, location of utterance, and time of utterance.

This is an interesting suggestion, which allows Sidelle to account for certain true instances of 'I am not here now' without postulating the existence of alternative characters for the indexical expressions at issue. It is not, however, entirely satisfactory. Consider this modification of the anecdote about Jones, who expects his wife to come home at 5 p.m., and writes at 8 a.m.

I am not here now, meet me in six hours

with the intention of informing Mrs Jones that she is to meet him at 11 p.m.—or, if you prefer, imagine that he records 'Meet me in six hours' on a tape, expecting his wife to activate the tape-recorder upon her arrival. However, Jones's wife is late, and she only reads the message (or turns on the tape-recorder) at 6 p.m. Clearly the vicissitudes of Mrs Jones do not affect the profile of her husband's message: she would simply *mis*interpret the note, were she to conclude that her husband will be waiting for her at the Cabo Real at midnight—that is, six hours from the actual decoding time. Intuitively, then, the message's interpretation is to be established with respect to the time of *expected* decoding, and not with respect to the time when decoding actually takes place. However, as I explain in the next paragraph, the Remote Utterance View seems unable to yield this pre-theoretically desired outcome.

Sidelle agrees with the conclusion that the temporal indexicals in Jones's message indicate 5 p.m. as the time of his absence, and 11 p.m. as the time of the prospective meeting, but he believes this conclusion to be compatible with his theory, once it is amended along the following lines:

> Two proposals suggest themselves here. One would be to say that the referents of 'here' and 'now' are given by the intended, or maybe expected, location and time of the utterance.... This may differ only verbally from the second tack, which would say that there are parameters set when making deferring utterances upon the situations in which the deferred utterances may occur. (Sidelle 1991: 537)

These suggestions deserve a closer look. The first proposal, which holds that the referents of the indexicals in cases such as Jones's are obtained with respect to the intended or expected location and time of utterance, is silent with respect to Jones's genuine utterance. It may thus be developed in two different directions:

(A) Jones's genuine utterance takes place in Jones's house at 5 p.m. Then, the simple-minded index—namely, the index containing the parameters of utterance—includes Jones's house and 5 p.m. Hence, consistent with Sidelle's commitment to the Simple-Minded View, 'now' or 'in six hours' manage to refer to the desired intervals.

(B) Jones's genuine utterance does not take place in Jones's house at 5 p.m.; it occurs at some other time, presumably at 6 p.m., when Mrs Jones reads the note, or perhaps it does not take place at all. Given that, as intuitions and Sidelle concur, 'here' and 'now' refer to Jones's house and to 5 p.m., this entails that indexical expressions are not inevitably to be evaluated with respect to the context of genuine utterance—i.e., that, contrary to the Simple-Minded View, the index appropriate to certain instances is distinct from the simple-minded index.

View (A) does not seem to be a viable solution: it is implausible to hold that, in the story of Jones, a genuine utterance occurs at 5 p.m., when in fact no interesting event whatsoever is taking place at that time. The note, you may recall, was written at eight in the morning, and is not being read until six in the evening: at five, it just lies there unread, just as it did at four and will continue to do at 5.30. And (A) is most likely not what Sidelle had in mind, since he writes that his first suggestion 'may differ only verbally' from his 'second tack'. According to Sidelle's second proposal, Jones's deferral misfires: since no relevant event takes place within the intended parameters, no genuine utterance occurs at all. This suggestion, far from being only verbally different from (A), is incompatible with it. It is, however, compatible with (B), which does not rule out the possibility that no genuine utterance took place in the story of Jones. However, not unlike version (B) of the first view, the 'second tack' entails the rejection of the Simple-Minded View. Otherwise, the 'second tack' would have to conclude that the indexical expressions occurring in Jones's note lack any referent whatsoever. Such a conclusion is intuitively incorrect, and it is incompatible with Sidelle's insight that 'now' and 'in six hours' in Jones's note refer to 5 and 11 p.m.

3. Beyond Recorded Messages

In sections 1 and 2, I suggested that examples of written notes and recorded speech involving indexical expressions support the rejection of the Simple-Minded View—that is, I argued that they are appropriately represented by taking into consideration an index distinct from the simple-minded index (and that, on the basis of such representation, they are suitably evaluated by interpretive systems such as that from section 1). But, as I hinted above, recorded messages are by no means the only evidence for this conclusion. In this section, I present a variety of examples in which no 'device for later broadcast' is involved, that may not be treated in the intuitively correct fashion by the Simple-Minded View.[6]

Consider first a passage from Wolfgang Hildesheimer's book on Mozart, written around 1976:

> In the summer of 1829 Aloysia Lange, née Weber, visits Mary Novello in her hotel room in Vienna.... Aloysia, the once celebrated singer, now an old lady of sixty-seven ... gives Mary the impression of a broken woman lamenting her fate, not without tears. (Hildesheimer 1982: 97)

Clearly, Hildesheimer is not making the patently false claim that Aloysia Lange is 67 in 1976, and that she is then giving Mary Novello the impression of a broken woman. Figuratively speaking, he is positioning himself at the time of the described events, and is narrating Aloysia's situation from the 'point of view' of 1829. On the assumption that 'now' is associated with its customary character, and on the assumption of an interpretive system along the lines summarized in Chapter 1, it follows that the above passage is to be interpreted with respect to an index which, unlike the simple-minded index, contains 1829 as its temporal co-ordinate.[7]

It may be complained that 'now' in Hildesheimer's passage is within the influence of the temporal operator 'In the summer of

---

[6] For a discussion of other cases, see also Predelli 1996. For a treatment of similar examples accompanied by an analysis of related phenomena see Schlenker 2004. See also Bianchi 2001a; Corazza 2004; Corazza et al. 2002; Recanati 2002a; and Vision 1985.

[7] Note that the verbs occurring in the passage are in the *present* tense. The phenomenon instantiated by this example is thus importantly different from the use of 'now' exemplified in narrative contexts by past-tense sentences such as 'Now she felt at home'. Kamp and Reyle have suggested that examples of this latter kind indicate that 'now' is anchored to what they call the 'temporal perspective point', rather than to the time of utterance (see Kamp and Reyle 1993: 595–6 and 612). But since in present-tense examples such as the one under discussion Kamp and Reyle's temporal perspective point coincides with utterance time (Kamp and Reyle 1993: 596), I may safely ignore this distinction for the purpose of this essay.

54 ~ *Systems and Indexes*

1829', occurring at the beginning of the fragment under discussion. In this view, the vicissitudes of 'now' may be modelled on those of, for instance, a definite description. So, 'the president of the United States in the summer of 1829' does not denote the current president, precisely because the effect of the operator shifts the temporal anchor to the indicated time. Similarly, in this approach, when 'now' occurs within the scope of that expression, it ends up referring to the time indicated by the operator, rather than to the index's temporal co-ordinate. But this suggestion is misguided: indexical expressions continue to select the appropriate contextual item even when occurring in a sentence affected by intensional operators (see Kaplan 1977). For instance, 'In 2005, those who are rich now will be poor' does not predict the existence of prosperous destitutes in 2005: even when embedded within the scope of 'In 2005', 'now' persists in its relation to the index's parameter.

I am also unconvinced by the objection that 'now' in Hildesheimer's narrative manages to pick up the appropriate time in virtue of an *anaphoric* link to the discourse-initial expression 'In the summer of 1829'—or, at least, I am unconvinced that, in the sense in which I find it intelligible, this proposal is indeed an objection to my view. As commonly understood, anaphora is a relation between expressions: an expression e anaphoric on an antecedent expression e^* is interpreted by virtue of some systematic relation with the evaluation appropriate for e^*. In this sense, however, it is difficult to understand how anaphora can provide an explanation for the phenomenon under discussion here, since explicit mention of the appropriate date does not appear to be at all necessary for the relevant interpretation of the present tense or the temporal indexicals. In an appropriate setting, I may, for instance, successfully begin my narration of Aloysia's past misfortunes with 'Aloysia, now an old lady of sixty-seven, gives Mary the impression of a broken woman', without resorting to expressions overtly indicating the salient temporal location. On an extended conception of anaphora, 'now' may well turn out to be 'anaphorically' linked to appropriate extra-linguistic items, such as the intended time of evaluation. Yet, leaving aside the dubious merit of extending the term 'anaphora' in this way, what this suggestion amounts to is merely the claim that, if the desired results are to be obtained, 'now' must end up referring to 1829, rather than to the time of writing. This much, indeed, is by no means an objection to my approach.

It is also not too difficult to come up with analogous examples involving indexical expressions that address the location parameter of the index. Take the following passages from *California, The Ultimate Guidebook* (Riegert 1990). In the chapter on Los Angeles, we read:

If an entire neighbourhood could qualify as an outdoor museum, the Mount Washington district would probably charge admission. Here, just northwest of downtown, are several picture-book expressions of desert culture within a few blocks. (Riegert 1990: 37)

Later, we find this description of the Coast Starlight train-route to Santa Barbara:

Picking up the baton in Los Angeles, the 'Coast Starlight' continues north and west to the Pacific, shuttling past stretches of open water populated with surfers and occasional fishermen. Here the tracks hone a fine line along sharp rockfaces. (Riegert 1990: 238)

It may safely be assumed that Ray Riegert, the author of the guidebook, wrote it in his house. But this assumption surely does not entail that the above passages must be interpreted as asserting that expressions of desert culture occur in Riegert's home, or that train tracks hone a fine line along sharp rockfaces in his residence. The writer intends that his remarks be interpreted with respect to Mount Washington and the Southern California coastline. As a result, the correct interpretation of his inscriptions is obtained by feeding the interpretive system with representations involving appropriate indexes: namely, indexes which, unlike the simple-minded index, contain places distinct from the place of writing as their location parameters.

Note, incidentally, that neither the Many Characters View nor the Remote Utterance View fare well here. In particular, the distinction between 'now$_{DT}$' and 'now$_{ET}$' and its analogue for spatial indexicals is inapplicable to the foregoing examples. 'Now' in the passage on Aloysia refers neither to the time of encoding (when the book was written), nor to the time of decoding (when I read it), and 'here' in the excerpts on California picks up neither the author's home nor the location of the reader. The Many Characters View could take such instances into account only by associating the indexical expressions at issue with new characters, devised in an *ad hoc* fashion in order to obtain the desired interpretations.[8]

There are also straightforward examples involving agent indexicals. Consider, for instance, the case of a lecturer commenting on the *Nicomachean Ethics* in an introductory class. She says:

I argued at length that one lives the best life by exercising both moral and intellectual virtues. And now I am suddenly advocating a rather different position, namely that the good life must be devoted solely to theoretical activity. Do you see a way out of this apparent inconsistency?

The lecturer is not presenting her own prima-facie incompatible opinions on human life. She is temporarily pretending to be in Aristotle's shoes, and she employs the first person pronoun to refer to him, rather than to herself. Once again, the appropriate representation of her remarks must include an index distinct from the simple-minded index, this time with respect to its

---

[8] For instance, according to Smith, the occurrence of 'now' in cases similar to the Hildesheimer passage is 'governed by the rule that it refers to the historical time the speaker wishes to emphasise and take as his chronological point of reference' (Smith 1989: 172).

agent co-ordinate. Given an index containing Aristotle, rather than the speaker, the correct results are obtained in a straightforward manner, on the basis of the indexicals' customary characters, and of the obvious procedures of the system from Chapter 1.[9]

4. I Am Here Now

If the analysis defended thus far is on the right track, a variety of examples are appropriately represented from the interpretive system's point of view by means of pairs involving an index distinct from the simple-minded index. To a great extent, my rejection of the Simple-Minded View falls squarely within what Quine called 'preparatory operations': namely, the set of hypotheses on the basis of which particular utterances (or inscriptions) are regimented in the canonical format acceptable for the purpose of semantic interpretation. It would then seem that, whether I am right or not about written notes or the historic present, nothing of relevance follows from my approach when it comes to the system's inner workings. Indeed, as I stressed above, it is a consequence of the analysis I defended that, once the appropriate clause–index pair has been identified, the indexicals proceed with their customary characters, and results of truth-value are obtained on the basis of the usual mechanisms of compositional analysis.

Still, the reason why I paused on questions of representation is not entirely without relevance to this essay's main topic, the view of meaning and truth entailed by the traditional approach. To the contrary, the examples I discussed serve the pedagogical purpose of bringing to light certain important features of some of the parameters at work 'inside' the interpretive system's machinery:

[9] For further comments on 'I' see Corazza *et al*. 2002.

namely, indexes. The discussion of the role which indexes play within a system is particularly urgent because, as I explain in what follows, even the foremost defenders of the traditional paradigm have misunderstood the relationship between indexes and *contexts*, understood as the particular situations in which an utterance takes place. As a consequence, traditional systems have been burdened with inadequate commitments, in particular when it comes to the assessment of logical truth, or, as it is sometimes called, 'truth in virtue of meaning'.

As I explained, the Simple-Minded View assumes that the context in which an utterance takes place straightforwardly supplies the co-ordinates for the index involved in that utterance's representation. Indexes, on this view, inevitably include the utterer, and the location, time, and world at which the utterance under analysis takes place. If this is the case, it seems inevitable that indexes end up borrowing certain important features from the structure of contexts, in particular when it comes to the mutual relationships between their co-ordinates. Suppose, for instance, that you insist that, for reasons of metaphysical necessity or whatever other motive, an utterer is always at the location of utterance when her utterance takes place. Then, given the notion that indexes reflect contexts in the obvious manner sanctioned by the Simple-Minded View, you might very naturally conclude that such presumed regularities trickle down to a constraint on the index's structure: for any index $i = <i_A, i_L, i_T, i_W, \ldots>$, where i_A, i_L, i_T, and i_W are, respectively, the index's agent, location, time, and world co-ordinates, i_A must be in i_L at time i_T in world i_W. Or assume that, for one reason or another, it turns out that the speaker must always exist at the time of utterance. In the spirit of the Simple-Minded View, it follows that, if any n-tuple $<i_A, i_L, i_T, i_W, \ldots>$ is to qualify as an index, it must be such that i_A exists in i_W at i_T.

It is not crucial whether the aforementioned assumptions regarding contexts, such as the notion that the speaker is at the contextual location at the time of utterance, are indeed correct. Perhaps, consonant with Sidelle's rejection of premiss (d) in section 1, cases of 'remote utterances' indicate the non-inevitability of the suggestions from the foregoing paragraph. (Note, incidentally, that my criticism of Sidelle does not amount to a denial that speakers may indeed perform remote utterance. The point is merely that such a notion is not the central tool in the analysis of the examples of section 1.) What is important here, rather, is the discussion of the relation between whatever hypothesis one may be willing to accept pertaining to contexts of utterance, and the structure and function of indexes within the interpretive system. What is at issue, in other words, is the notion that, in the development of one's favourite systems, indexes are supposed to borrow certain presumed characteristics of contexts of utterance.

The notion that a speaker is at the location of her utterance when she is producing it is, albeit implicitly, widely accepted. Given the further notion that 'I', 'here', and 'now' refer to the utterer, and the place and location at which the utterance takes place, it follows that sentences such as 'I am here now' are always truly utterable; i.e., they are *warrantedly utterable*. So, Simon Blackburn, to cite just one among many, insists that '[t]he sentence "I am here" has the peculiar property that whenever I utter it, it is bound to be true' (Blackburn 1984: 334). Given a conclusion of this kind, theorists interested in the details responsible for such presumed peculiarity, notably David Kaplan, have developed their semantic approaches on the basis of assumptions intended to reflect the aforementioned alleged regularity. Interestingly, in Kaplan's view, the collections of the parameters relevant for the evaluation of indexical expressions—that is, what I have called 'indexes'—are labelled as 'context', and are constrained in a manner reminiscent of the alleged structure characteristic of 'contexts', in the everyday sense of the term. Thus, in his interpretive system for the indexical language *LD*, Kaplan explicitly restricts the class of indexes to quadruples

$<w, x, p, t>$ 'such that in the world w, x is located at p at the time t', and such that x exists in w at t (Kaplan 1977: 509; see also p. 544). Following Kaplan, I refer to n-tuples of this kind as *proper* indexes. Clearly, the (clauses corresponding to) the sentences 'I am here now' and 'I exist' turn out to be true with respect to every proper index. Hence, given Kaplan's decision to restrict the system's attention to indexes of this type, it is an outcome of the system's compositional analysis that these expressions turn out to be true at all indexes *simpliciter*, and hence as logically true. In a passage in which intuitions of warranted utterability are intermingled with questions of logic, Kaplan concludes that

['I am here now'] is deeply, and in some sense... universally, true. One need only understand the meaning of [it] to know that it cannot be uttered falsely.... [Our decision to accept only proper contexts] has the consequence that ['I am here now'] comes out, correctly, to be logically true. (Kaplan 1977: 509)[10]

Given the considerations of the previous sections in this chapter, there are many reasons to be unsatisfied with a conclusion of this kind. To begin with, the possibility that at least some examples may involve Sidelle's 'remote utterances' seems to cast doubt on the notion that a speaker is always at the place of utterance when her utterance occurs. Thus, even if the Simple-Minded View were on the right track, there would be semantically relevant contexts such that the speaker is not at the contextual location at the time of utterance. More importantly, as I explained, the Simple-Minded View is *not* on the right track: even leaving aside cases possibly explainable by means of Sidelle's apparatus, other examples indicate that their correct interpretation must be obtained by appealing to *improper* indexes—that is, indexes i such that i_A is not in i_L at i_T and i_W. For example, the correct index for Jones's note (2) contains Jones, Jones's home,

---

[10] For this definition of logical validity, see Kaplan 1977: 547.

and the expected time of his wife's arrival, five o'clock, as, respectively, the agent, location, and temporal parameter. Yet, Jones is not at home at five o'clock, his absence being the very reason why he had to resort to written notes in order to communicate with his wife. Worse still, Jones might not even exist at five o'clock, were he to die, say, on his way to the airport.

But a further comment is appropriate at this stage. The analysis I proposed of cases such as (2) indicates that, as a matter of fact, 'I am here now' is not warrantedly utterable; i.e., it *can* be uttered falsely. In other words, it so happens that there exist particular instances, whose representations involve improper indexes—so that the decision to restrict the system's attention to proper indexes turns out to yield empirically inadequate results. But leave aside momentarily this rather obvious reason for rejecting Kaplan's restriction on the class of admissible indexes, and suppose that 'I am here now' is such that, indeed, it 'cannot be uttered falsely'. Is it the case that 'one need only understand the meaning' of the relevant expressions, in order to understand this example's presumed privileged status? I do not think so. In what follows I argue that, even if Kaplan were right about what may or may not be uttered falsely, the alleged regularities constraining what Kaplan appropriately calls 'the vagaries of actions' may not interfere with the 'verities of meaning' which the system is supposed to unveil (Kaplan 1989: 584–5).

This conclusion may emerge with greater clarity by contrasting two different cases of validity yielded within Kaplan's system: on the one hand, the (formal counterpart of) 'I am here now', and on the other hand, another case (correctly) presented as an example of the type of validity characteristic of indexical languages, namely instances of

(5) (actually φ) if and only if φ.

Incidentally, it should be noted that my agreement that examples of the latter type *do* qualify as logical truths preserves one of the most important philosophical consequences of Kaplan's interpretive system: namely, the unsoundness of the rule of necessitation (if p is logically true, so is 'necessarily p'). For 'it is necessary that ((actually φ) if and only if φ)' does (correctly) not turn out valid in Kaplan's system. Returning to the contrast with 'I am here now', compare the following arguments for the relevant conclusions of logical validity. As for (5), it is a consequence of Kaplan's treatment of 'actually' (and of the suggestion in the system of Chapter 1) that[11]

(a) 'actually φ' is true (i, t, w) iff φ is true (i, t, i_W),

where 'true (i, t, w)' abbreviates 'true with respect to an index i, a time t and a possible world w'. (I ignore assignments of values to variables for the sake of simplicity.) Thus, for any i,

(b) 'actually φ' is true (i, i_T, i_W) iff φ is true (i, i_T, i_W).

So, by the definition of 'if and only if', for any i,

(c) 'actually φ if and only if φ' is true (i, i_T, i_W).

Since being true (i, i_T, i_W) for all i is the requirement for validity, it follows (both in Kaplan's system and in the system of Chapter 1) that sentences of the form 'actually φ if and only if φ' are valid. Notice that the result in (c) appeals solely to the clauses for 'actually' and 'if and only if'. In particular, the only requirement on the structure of an index relevant for the reasoning to (c) is that indexes contain a possible world co-ordinate; i.e., that they be at least sufficiently rich to provide an evaluation for sentences involving 'actually'. Thus, sentences of the form 'actually φ if and only if φ' turn out to be true solely *in virtue of the meaning* of 'actually' and 'if and only if' (or, at least, in virtue of that portion of their meaning which is reflected in the

---

[11] Hereafter, I omit the parenthesis in '(actually φ) iff φ' for readability's sake. Note also that I employ single quotation marks instead of the more appropriate (but typographically cumbersome) corner-quotes.

interpretive system). The case is importantly different with respect to 'I am here now'. Given the customary characters for 'I', 'here', and 'now', and a sensible account of 'am' (in the sense of being located), the available conclusion is that

(d) 'I am here now' is true (i, t, w) iff i_A is in i_L at i_T in w.

So, for any i,

(e) 'I am here now' is true (i, i_T, i_W) iff i_A is in i_L at i_T in i_W.

But this conclusion does not entail that 'I am here now' is valid, unless it is antecedently stipulated, as it is by Kaplan, that indexes be such that, for any i, i_A is in i_L at i_T in i_W.

The arguments from the foregoing paragraph appeal to certain theses about 'I', 'am', 'actually', etc. intended to reflect salient aspects of their meaning. Whether these theses are at all correct is not immediately relevant here. What matters, rather, is that, once a certain account of 'actually' and 'if and only if' is taken for granted, a result of truth at all indexes is immediately forthcoming for cases such as (5). The same can not be said for 'I am here now', however. In this case, an important premiss must be accepted, in addition to the hypotheses regarding the meanings of 'I', 'am', 'here', and 'now': the indexes which the system may take into consideration must be proper indexes. It seems clear that such an assumption is not warranted by the conventional meaning of any expression. But if a doubt ensues in this respect, the examples from sections 2 and 3 provide definitive support for such a conclusion: it is not only the case that, in principle, improper indexes are to be considered within the interpretive system; it is also the case that, as a matter of fact, a variety of utterances do indeed require such indexes for their representation.

One final comment on a related remark by Kaplan on logical truth. Kaplan argues that his treatment of indexical languages 'brings a new perspective' on indexical-free sentences such as 'something exists' (see Kaplan 1977: 548). In Kaplan's formalism, 'something exists' is rendered as '$\exists x$ Exist x'. About this sentence, Kaplan remarks:

> in [the Logic of Demonstratives] such sentences as '$\exists x$ Exist x'... are valid, although they would not be so regarded in traditional logic. At least not in the neotraditional logic that countenances empty worlds. (Kaplan 1977: 549)

(Of course, '$\exists x$ Exist x' is recognized as valid in customary treatments, due to the explicit prohibition of empty domains. But it is not this feature that Kaplan highlights, but the presumed fact that, even once this prohibition is bracketed away, the example turns out to be valid in virtue of the peculiarities of what he calls the 'Logic of Demonstratives'.) Kaplan presents his conclusion as an outcome of the fact that

> it is not the case that each possible circumstance is part of a possible context. In particular, the fact that each possible context has an agent implies that any possible circumstance in which no individuals exist will not form a part of any possible context. (Kaplan 1977: 549)

In the terminology of my essay, Kaplan's reasoning may be summarized as follows. Every admissible index i contains an agent i_A, such that i_A exists at the time and world of i. Thus, something exists at the time and world of i. Hence, for any index i, at least one individual exists in i_W at i_T. Hence, '$\exists x$ Exist x' is true (i, i_T, i_W) for all i; i.e., it is valid. The restriction of indexes to proper indexes, of course, is at work in the very first step of the foregoing argument.

It is hardly surprising that Kaplan's conclusion of logical truth is obtainable only on the independent assumption of a restricted class of admissible indexes. What is at issue with '$\exists x$ Exist x' is not the evaluation of any indexical *expression*: the 'Logic of Demonstratives' is now understood as an apparatus involving relativization to indexes, but in this particular case uninterested in the vicissitudes of 'I', 'now', or 'here'. But if the language at issue is, or may well be, an indexical-free fragment, it would be puzzling if the conclusions reached by its analysis were able to unveil new results of truth in virtue of *meaning*. Indeed, they do not. At least within the 'neotraditional logic that countenances empty worlds', 'something exists' follows the fate of 'I am here now': both manage to obtain their privileged status only on the basis of the illegitimate restriction of admissible indexes to proper indexes.

That 'I am not here now' and the other examples discussed above should not come out as true at all indexes is a conclusion forcefully brought to light by my rejection of the Simple-Minded View, and by the considerations regarding the representation of particular utterances in the previous section. But regardless of how things happen to be with respect to the interface between systems and utterances, the notion that 'I am here now' is inevitably true is grounded on the erroneous attraction to the vagaries of actions for the purpose of semantic interpretation. The relationship between 'vagaries' and 'verities' continues to be a central theme in the next chapter, where I discuss the so-called token-reflexive approach to indexicality. But before concluding this chapter, I will add a few remarks pertaining to the consequences of my rejection of the Simple-Minded View with respect to fictional discourse.

5. Talk about Fiction

Suppose that we are discussing Milos Forman's film *Amadeus*, and that I say

(6) Salieri commissioned the *Requiem*.

My utterance is apparently true: in the film, the composer Antonio Salieri *is* the mysterious figure who anonymously commissions the Mass for the Dead. Imagine now that I utter (6) during a debate on the history of sacred music in eighteenth-century Vienna. My utterance appears to be false: the *Requiem* was probably commissioned by Count Walsegg, surely not by *Kappelmeister* Salieri (see Robbins Landon 1988). But how can an utterance of an indexical-free sentence such as (6) (matters of tense aside) be true when it occurs in a conversation about a film, yet be false when it is part of my comment on the history of music? And, more generally, how can an utterance of (6) be true at all, given that Salieri did *not* commission the *Requiem*?

Suppose, as seems plausible, that it is the interpretive system's responsibility to yield corresponding verdicts of truth-value for the clause–index pair(s) appropriate to the utterances in question. So, what is needed is a result of truth in one case and of falsehood in the other. Given the structure of traditional systems, it apparently follows that *two* distinct clause–index pairs must be at issue. But questions pertaining to the interpretation of indexical expressions do not appear to be immediately relevant with respect to the issue under discussion. Hence, so it is often concluded, the relevant distinction between the representations for the aforementioned utterances must have to do with the *clauses* appropriate in each of them. A typical example of how one may proceed on the basis of this conclusion is offered by what I call the 'Hidden Operator Project', or Hop for short.

Although different versions of Hop have been proposed, in its simplest form this suggestion insists that my utterance about the actual course of Austrian musical history may be taken at face value, and be represented by a syntactic construct closely corresponding to the uttered sentence (*modulo* whatever level of syntactic complexity one deems to be independently required). My other utterance, on the other hand, must involve a clause reflecting a structure roughly such as

(7) It is true in the film *Amadeus* that Salieri commissioned the *Requiem*.

Writing in this spirit, David Lewis insists that examples such as my commentary on the movie are 'abbreviations for longer sentences beginning with an operator "in such-and-such fiction" ' (Lewis 1978: 37). Hartry Field writes that ' "Santa Claus flies reindeer" is true only when it is elliptical for "The story says that Santa Claus flies reindeer" ' (Field 1973: 471 n. 8). And for Michael Devitt, 'a statement about fiction is (usually) implicitly preceded by a fiction operator roughly paraphrasable by... "in fiction".... suppose I assert ["Tom Jones is illegitimate"], then my token is paraphrasable by "F(Tom Jones is illegitimate)" ' (Devitt 1981: 172).

On this view, then, falsehood is straightforwardly obtainable for the clause-index appropriate to my factual remark, given that Salieri, the referent of 'Salieri', is not within the actual extension of the predicate 'commissioned the *Requiem*'. As for my other statement, it is to be expected that a sufficiently ingenuous treatment of the locution 'It is true in the film *Amadeus* that' occurring in the appropriate clause may yield the desired truth-value, truth, for the clause–index pair in question. In 'Truth in Fiction', David Lewis has suggested a treatment of expressions such as 'in fiction f (it is true that)' as intensional operators, along the following lines:

a prefixed sentence 'In fiction f, φ' is true... iff φ is true at every possible world in a certain set, this set being somehow determined by the fiction f. (Lewis 1978: 39)

Assume whatever tenable account you prefer of the relationships between a piece of fiction and a certain class of worlds. No matter what the details of such an account turn out to be, and regardless of how it handles certain tricky examples, it seems that the sentence occurring within the scope of the intensional operator in (7) is true at every world 'determined' by the film *Amadeus*: had things gone as the film recounts, 'Salieri commissioned the *Requiem*' would have turned out to be true. Thus, so Hop concludes, the clause–index type appropriate to my utterance about the film is evaluated as true by any suitable interpretive system, as intuitively desired.

The foregoing story needs considerable sharpening, in particular when it comes to the analysis of a story and of the class of worlds it 'determines'. Still, I am optimistic in this respect, and I am willing to concede that no insurmountable obstacles hinder the development of an acceptable theory in this direction. In what follows, I shall thus join the Hop theorist in the conviction that a satisfactory solution to the semantic puzzle discussed in this section may safely rely on the notion of the fiction's associated possible world (or class of such worlds). The reason why I am not entirely satisfied with Hop has rather to do with more directly 'linguistic' issues, in particular pertaining to the justification for its choice of the clause relevant to one of the utterances under discussion. Why, leaving aside the fact that Hop eventually obtains the desired result, are we to suppose that my remark about the movie is to be represented by means of a clause including an expression that I not only failed to utter, but in all likelihood did not even take into consideration at all? In what sense is my utterance, or the sentence I uttered, 'elliptical for' or an 'abbreviation of' the longer expression that Hop aims at evaluating?[12]

The absence of satisfactory replies to these questions does not suffice as an *argument* against Hop. In what follows, I rest satisfied with the weaker conclusion that, given the theoretical apparatus developed for examples such as those in sections 1 and 2 in this chapter, the strategy implemented by Hop is not necessary. Independently motivated conclusions, so I argue, provide a natural analysis of the case discussed in this section.

Recall the examples of Aloysia Langer, the once celebrated singer, and of the lecturer discussing the *Nichomachean Ethics*. In those cases, it seemed natural to suppose that the speaker (or writer) was, in a sense, looking at matters 'from the point of view of her subject matter', be it the year 1829 or Aristotle. By the same token, when discussing *Amadeus*, I was, roughly speaking,

[12] For a criticism of Hop in this vein, see Bertolet 1984.

talking 'from the point of view of the story'. When this vague insight is developed within the apparatus I have suggested, it points towards the conclusion that my utterance about the film, not unlike the examples in section 3, be represented by a pair containing an index other than the simple-minded index. In this case, the parameter which differentiates the appropriate index from the simple-minded index is the possible world co-ordinate: the index with respect to which my utterance is evaluated does not contain the world in which it took place, i.e., the actual world, but 'the world' of the story. Some considerations pertaining to the interpretation of the modal indexical 'actually', parallel to the considerations in section 3 about 'now' and 'I', seem to indicate that this suggestion is on the right track. Suppose that, while talking about the film, I say

> (8) Although Mozart thought that the mysterious figure was his father's ghost, the actual commissioner of the *Requiem* was Salieri.

Given how things are described in the film, this utterance is intuitively true. But in order to obtain the correct interpretation for 'the actual commissioner', (8) must be evaluated with respect to an index containing the fictional world of *Amadeus* as its world parameter. With respect to such an index, 'The actual commissioner of the *Requiem*' denotes Salieri, and the sentence 'The actual commissioner of the *Requiem* was Salieri' comes out true. But with respect to the world in which my utterance takes place—that is, with respect to the world parameter in the simple-minded index—'the actual commissioner of the *Requiem*' denotes Count Walsegg, and 'The actual commissioner of the *Requiem* was Salieri' is, wrongly, evaluated as false.[13]

---

[13] Note that my discussion of the example of *Amadeus* assumes that 'actual' is indexically anchored to the index's possible-world parameter; for a defence of this view, see Salmon 1987. See also Lewis 1970.

At the beginning of this section, I sketched a reasoning leading towards a 'hidden operator' approach to the puzzle under discussion. That reasoning started with the (correct) assumption that interpretive systems ought to yield contrasting results of truth-value for my utterances of (6), and that, consequently, they must take into consideration distinct clause–index pairs. From this premiss, it proceeded by pointing out that, since (6) does not contain indexical expressions (leaving aside the irrelevant issue of the verbal tense), a distinction of indexes would not yield the desired evaluational discrepancy. Focusing on the clauses appropriate to each utterance was thus left as the only viable option. But the second premiss in this argument, pertaining to the role that indexes play within the interpretive system, is incorrect: as already hinted in Chapter 1, and as explained in greater detail in the following paragraphs, indexes are relevant not only to the evaluation of indexical expressions, but also to the establishment of unrelativized truth-value.

Consider my utterance of

(9) Bill Clinton was the United States President in 1995.

In straightforward instances—that is, in cases where the simple-minded index is appropriate for my utterance's representation—a result of Truth is obtained by the system whenever the pair made up of the appropriate clause and the aforementioned index turns out to be mapped to truth at the actual world. Informally, my utterance is false with respect to merely counterfactual circumstances, such as a scenario in which a Republican was President in 1995 or a setting in which the United States is a monarchy. Still, it is true *tout court* because, given how things actually went with American politics, the actual world corresponds to a point with respect to which the appropriate t-distribution yields a result of truth. But consider now the possible utterance of (9) which I *would* have performed, had it been the case that George Bush Sr won the 1992 election. Would that

Systems and Indexes ~ 71

utterance of mine have been true, or would I have been speaking falsely? Clearly, my counterfactual utterance must be mapped to the same t-distribution by an appropriate system as the aforementioned actual utterance; i.e., the one is true with respect to a point iff the other is. Yet, unlike my actual utterance, my counterfactual utterance is intuitively false *simpliciter*, since it is false with respect to what would have been the actual world, had Bush Sr been able to defeat his opponent.

What this indicates is that a verdict of unrelativized truth may be obtained, informally speaking, by taking into consideration the 'contextually appropriate' circumstances—i.e., more precisely, the point of evaluation determined by the appropriate index. Compare the indexes for the two utterances of (9) described above. They differ with respect to (at least) the world parameter: in the case of my actual utterance, the actual world, in the case of the utterance I would have made had the Republican candidate won the 1992 election, a world in which Bush Sr rules the United States in 1995. More generally, then, and in the more austere terminology of Chapter 1, an utterance represented by means of a clause–index pair $<s, i>$ turns out True iff $<s, i>$ is evaluated as true with respect to the point determined by i—i.e., with respect to $<i_W, i_T>$.

That indexes play a role within the system over and above that appropriate to the evaluation of indexical expressions not only highlights the problem in the customary reasoning favouring Hop, but also hints at a more natural solution to the puzzle under discussion. For it seems natural (and, moreover, consistent with the argument about the interpretation of 'actually' in cases such as (8)) to conclude that the representation appropriate to my utterance about the film does not involve the simple-minded index, but rather an index that contains the world of the movie as its world co-ordinate. It follows from this thesis, together with the classic definition of truth, that my cinematographic remark is true *simpliciter* iff it is true at the world of *Amadeus*; i.e., iff according to the film Salieri commissioned the *Requiem*. On the other hand, of course, my utterance of (6) as a factual remark is represented by means of an index including the actual world as its world co-ordinate—in all likelihood, the simple-minded index. As desired, this case turns out to be false *simpliciter*, given that the *Requiem* was actually commissioned by Count Walsegg, and not by Salieri.[14]

6. Where Am I Now?

In Chapter 1, I explained that the suitable inputs for traditional interpretive systems are abstract items of a particular kind, clause–index pairs. In this chapter, I paused on questions pertaining to the choice of the index appropriate to the representation of certain utterances (or inscriptions) in a format of this type. I argued that the Simple-Minded View is incorrect, and that some examples are suitably interpreted by considering an index containing parameters other than the speaker, or the time, location, and possible world at which they occur. I then employed my rejection of the Simple-Minded View as additional evidence against independently incorrect restrictions often imposed on the class of indexes relevant from the system's point of view. Even if the Simple-Minded View were on the right track, so I argued, the restriction of indexes to proper indexes would yield undesirable results of 'truth in virtue of meaning', and would inappropriately absorb within the system's structure regularities affecting the process of utterance. That the Simple-Minded View is *not* on the right track provides conclusive evidence in this respect: in particular instances, indexicals may actually be used

---

[14] It should be pointed out that the approach defended here is idle with respect to a quite distinct semantic problem related to discourse about fiction, pertaining to the semantic behaviour of so-called fictional names, such as 'Holmes'. On this topic, see Salmon 1998 and my Predelli 2002*a*.

so as to refer to items distinct from those provided by the simple-minded index.

Before concluding this chapter, I wish to pause on another consequence of the considerations put forth thus far having to do with the distinction between 'pure' indexicals and demonstratives, and with some of the comments with which I concluded Chapter 1. According to Kaplan, indexical expressions such as 'I' and 'now' are pure indexicals: they are assigned a referent (or whatever type of semantic value they require) regardless of demonstrations, acts of pointing, or intentional involvement on the speaker's behalf. Other indexicals are not of this kind: depending on your favourite view, demonstratives require an accompanying ostensive act, or the speaker's focused attention on a certain object, or some other factor along these lines. As hinted towards the end of Chapter 1, anti-traditionalist writers such as Recanati have pursued this line of thought, and have concluded that demonstratives, unlike pure indexicals, involve 'pragmatic' considerations, having to do with the speaker's intention or with questions of contextual relevance: at least for these cases, so they conclude, reference assignment is not guided by meaning alone.

The notion of 'automatic' interpretation assumed as appropriate for pure indexicals strikes me as hardly intelligible. From the interpretive system's point of view, in the cases of 'I' and 'that' alike, characters patiently sit and wait for the parameters with respect to which a result may be obtained. From the point of view of an application of the interpretive system to particular utterances, in the cases of 'I' and 'that' alike, what is at issue are representational questions uncontroversially independent of the expressions' meaning. This much emerges, for instance, from a comparison of Kaplan's 'Demonstratives' and 'Afterthoughts': Kaplan's change of mind about the interpretation of demonstratives does not (or at least need not) affect the structure of the interpretive system he proposes.

When it comes to Kaplan's suggestions pertaining to actual utterances (in the everyday sense of the term, and not in the technical sense of the term operative in 'Demonstratives'), of course, I disagree: as argued in sections 2 and 3, 'I' and 'now' are no less 'pragmatically promiscuous' than 'this' and 'that'. In other words, the distinction between pure indexicals and demonstratives, which clearly plays no role from the point of view of the system's inner workings, is also idle with respect to the representational issues involved in its application to particular instances. The direction of my denial of the pure indexical versus demonstrative distinction must surely appear surprising to Recanati-style anti-traditionalists: my staunchly traditionalist essay does not attempt to reduce presumably pragmatics-permeated demonstratives to formally tractable pure indexicals, but pursues the opposite strategy. That this approach is not only compatible with the traditional paradigm, but actually helps to unveil its true commitments with respect to meaning and truth, is one of the main conclusions of the present chapter.

Chapter 3
The Vagaries of Action

As indicated in Chapter 1, the interpretive system, paired with appropriate hypotheses of representation, yields results interpretable as conclusions about a given utterance. Given the assumption that an utterance *u* is perspicuously representable by means of the pair <*s, i*>, the system's assignment of a t-distribution to <*s, i*> may thus be compared with some of our intuitions about *u*. (Exactly what such intuitions are, and what relationships they bear to our pre-theoretic assessment of *u*'s truth-conditions, is a question that will be scrutinized more closely later in the book.) An approach along these lines follows the traditional assumption that a satisfactory systematic analysis of an utterance's semantic profile focuses on a certain complex expression-type, evaluated with respect to the parameters offered by the accompanying index. As for the choice of the latter item in the pair under analysis, the index, I discussed some perhaps not sufficiently appreciated issues in Chapter 2. Regarding the procedures leading to the identification of the type suited to the representation of a given utterance, I shall not add anything of significance to the few unsophisticated comments presented in the preceding chapters.

One related, general issue does, however, deserve more careful discussion. Following the by now classic Kaplan-inspired tradition, I supposed, and shall continue to suppose, that the system takes into consideration expression-types (hereinafter, ignoring for simplicity's sake the complexities involved in the appropriate clauses, English *sentence*-types), and evaluates them with respect to appropriate indexes. Yet, a view along these lines is at odds with a tendency which, though perhaps minority, is by no means unworthy of attention: namely, the notion that, when it comes to the study of indexical languages, the appropriate objects of analysis are tokens, interpreted by appealing to reflexive rules along the lines suggested by the so-called *token-reflexive* stance. The bulk of this chapter is devoted to token-reflexivity, and to my reasons for being less than satisfied with it.

My views in Chapter 2 pertaining to the choice of index suited to posted notes or passages in the historical present aimed at highlighting certain general conclusions relevant for the understanding of the structure and scope of traditional systems. In the same vein, the intended significance of my comments on token-reflexivity goes beyond mere assessment of the debate between token-oriented and more traditional treatments. What is ultimately at issue, here as in Chapter 2, is the relationship between meaning and truth offered by traditional systems, the resulting conclusions about logical properties, and the application of these results to actual instances of language use.

To anticipate, the view under scrutiny in this chapter, probably originating with Hans Reichenbach, claims that the semantic analysis of indexical languages ought to involve rules such as

> for any token *t* of 'now', *t* refers to the time when *t* was spoken;

that is, reflexive rules that apparently assign semantic properties to particular tokens, rather than to the expression-types they instantiate (see Reichenbach 1947). In his classic essay 'Demonstratives' (Kaplan 1977), Kaplan has argued against the Reichenbachian perspective, and has insisted that the inputs to the interpretive system be understood as what he calls 'sentences-in-context'. Recently, a number of semanticists, such as John Perry, Mark Crimmins, and especially Manuel Garcia-Carpintero, have challenged Kaplan's critique, and have defended a token-reflexive approach (see Perry 1997 and 2001; Crimmins 1995; Garcia-Carpintero 1998 and 2000).[1] In this chapter I argue that, although the considerations which Kaplan presents are not ultimately effective, other hints he provides may be developed into persuasive counter-arguments against token-reflexivity.

In section 1, I begin with a general presentation of the token-reflexive approach to indexical languages; in sections 2 and 3, I focus on issues pertaining to the validity of certain arguments and the status of certain sentences as logically true (true at all indexes). I begin by arguing on the token-reflexive theorist's behalf against certain only initially persuasive arguments favouring the traditional, non-reflexive approach, and I develop the conceptual apparatus needed for the study of the interface between token-reflexivity and matters of logic. In light of this background, I then present my argument against token-reflexivity, to the effect that views of this kind *overgenerate* with respect to logical truth: on a token-reflexive treatment, certain non-logically-true sentences turn out to be logically true.

In the final section, I turn to a different set of issues having to do with meaning, logical truth, and the truth-values of certain utterances. I discuss cases of logically true sentences whose utterances may well be (and in fact typically are) false, and of logically equivalent sentences whose utterances have intuitively distinct truth-values. For this purpose, I focus on the so-called puzzle of addressing, involving pronouns of formal addressing,

---

[1] Kaplan's direct criticism of Reichenbach in Kaplan 1977: 519—i.e., his argument against the thesis that 'I' is *synonymous* with 'the person who utters this token'—is of course widely accepted as uncontroversial, and is not relevant to the debate under discussion here.

and on cases of approximation, such as utterances of 'This table is 120 cm long' as descriptions of a 119.998 cm long table.

1. Preliminaries

When it comes to the debate discussed in this essay, the topic of contention is often presented in terms of a contrast between semanticists who take concrete tokens as the input for the interpretive system and those who favour an account focused on abstract expression-types. It should, however, be stressed at the outset that the debate in question is *not* primarily concerned with ontological issues pertaining to the existence or make-up of types or, more generally, of abstract entities. As for the sheer admissibility of expression-types, token-reflexive theorists are not only willing to *concede* the existence of repeatable types; they are also typically *committed* to the existence of objects of this kind, since, as we shall see, the rules they identify as steering the semantic behaviour of particular tokens appeal, among other things, to the expression-types they exemplify. On the other hand, the decision regarding the tenability of one view or another pertaining to the ontological make-up of types plays no role in the issues I shall address; neither token-reflexive theorists nor their critics are committed to particular accounts of what types are, and of what kind of metaphysical realm they inhabit. A telling example of such independence of ontological and semantic issues is provided by David Kaplan, one of the most outspoken critics of a token-reflexive treatment of indexicality, yet equally vocal against an understanding of the metaphysics of words as instantiable items, exemplified by their tokens in virtue of properties of shape or sound (see Kaplan 1990).[2]

---

[2] One ontological question that has a bearing on semantic issues is that pertaining to the understanding of tokens as events, rather than objects. The token of 'I am hungry now' written on a piece of paper may be employed by

It is not surprising that defenders of token-reflexive accounts have no interest in denying the admissibility and theoretical usefulness of repeatable types. A theory couched solely in terms of particular occurrences inevitably misses obvious and undeniably important regularities: my utterance of 'I am running now' uncontroversially displays a particular semantic profile in virtue of (among other things) the fact that it exemplifies a certain expression-type, one regulated by the conventions pertaining to the words I used. For this reason, one among the foremost defenders of the token-oriented approach, Manuel Garcia-Carpintero, explicitly declares his allegiance to what he correctly labels 'a platitude for everybody': namely, the notion that 'linguistic meanings are conventional, and therefore attach to repeatables—abstract expression types' (Garcia-Carpintero 2000: 37; see also Garcia-Carpintero 1998: 534).

On the other hand, equally unchallenged is the recognition that lone types do not suffice as inputs to a system able eventually to assign truth-values. Uncontroversially, whether an utterance of, say, 'I am running now' is true or false depends on a variety of aspects other than the type it exemplifies. Since what is needed, together with indications pertaining to the structure and composition of the type in question, is information regarding what is commonly called the context of utterance, type-theorists inevitably end up invoking structures consisting not of types alone, but of types paired with items appropriately related to contexts—in my terminology, clause(-types) paired with indexes. In the classic non-reflexive type-oriented approach, as I explained in the preceding chapters, given an index $i = <i_A, i_T, i_L, i_W>$, the system's evaluation of expression-types *vis-à-vis* indexes proceeds on the basis of rules such as, for instance,

the expression-type 'I' refers, with respect to an index i, to i_A.

different speakers at different times in order to achieve contrasting semantic effects (see Perry 1997 and Garcia-Carpintero 1998).

(This rule may be seen as the effect of combining the system's hypothesis pertaining to the character of 'I' with further claims regarding that expression's behaviour across points of evaluation: given an index i, the character of 'I' yields a function f such that, for any point p, $f(p) = i_A$.) Rules of this kind eventually yield results of unrelativized truth-value, such as the following:

> The sentence-type 'I am running now' is true with respect to an index i iff i_A is running at i_T in the possible world i_W.

These results may subsequently be applied to the evaluation of particular utterances, on the basis of appropriate hypotheses of representation, as discussed in Chapters 1 and 2.

As the foregoing paragraph indicates, commitment to an analysis focused on expression-types is compatible with the platitudes that lone sentence-types are not the bearers of semantic properties such as truth, and that any empirically adequate interpretive system ought to yield conclusions applicable to particular utterances. Token-reflexive theorists do not appear initially to require importantly different resources in this respect. Their views are committed not only to an appeal to expression-types within the rules steering the semantic behaviour of particular tokens: the additional elements they identify as relevant in this respect pertain, unsurprisingly enough, to contextual aspects parallel to those identified by their antagonists. For instance, Garcia-Carpintero (2000: 38–9) cites the following as a rule for 'I':

> For any token t of 'I', the referent of t is the speaker who has produced t.

Abstracting from the identification of the appropriate parameter as the person who is speaking (discussed in greater detail in Chapter 2), and rephrasing the rule in terms of formally tractable n-tuples, Garcia-Carpintero's proposal amounts to the notion that:

The Vagaries of Action ~ 81

> For any token t of 'I', the referent of t is i_A, where i is the index representing the context in which t takes place.

Similarly, once one reaches the stage relevant for the evaluation of entire sentences, token-reflexive accounts of indexicality may obtain conclusions presentable along the following lines:

> For any token t of 'I am running now', t is true iff i_A is running at time i_T in possible world i_W, where i is the index representing the context in which t takes place.

As I pointed out above, it is not only the case that the debate under analysis is independent of metaphysical issues pertaining to the nature of types or the admissibility of abstract entities. It is also true that, on either side of the dispute, (i) utterances are eventually associated with a certain semantic profile; (ii) such an association is driven, among other things, by hypotheses pertaining to the conventional meaning of the appropriate expression-types; and (iii) the semantic interpretation of an utterance must also involve hypotheses pertaining to the identification of the appropriate parameters, such as an agent or a time. However, these parallelisms notwithstanding, there seem to be significant differences between a token-reflexive approach to indexicality and more customary non-reflexive, type-oriented views. In the next two sections, I focus on some *prima-facie* plausible, but ultimately inadequate, suggestions in this respect. In section 4, I explain what I take to be a more important point of disagreement, pertaining to the role and structure played by indexes within token-reflexive theories, and, consequently, pertaining to the analysis of the logical profile of certain arguments and sentences.

2. Validity and Meaning

As explained in the previous section, semantic theories, be they systems of a traditional kind or theories of a token-reflexive orientation, yield conclusions of truth-value by taking into consideration sentence-types together with particular indexes. Given such assignment of truth-values, certain results inevitably follow pertaining to the relationships between different sentences, and hence to the validity of certain argumentative structures. These results are then amenable to intuitive scrutiny, at least as far as certain simple cases go: it is a constraint for any empirically adequate system that intuitively valid arguments are indeed recognized as such. One-premiss arguments such as the following appear to be prime candidates in this respect:

(1) I am running now. Therefore, I am running now.

Yet, it has occasionally been pointed out that token-reflexive accounts of 'now' are incompatible with the intuitive assessment of (1) as valid. At least in typical cases, it is the time of utterance (speaking, writing, etc.) that determines the appropriate index's time, and, at least in some situations, it is perfectly possible that the utterer stopped running right before the second token of 'now'. Thus, so this objection alleges, it follows from a token-reflexive account of 'now' that the temporal indexicals in (1) may be interpreted as making reference to two distinct times and that, when so interpreted, (1) may end up with a true premiss and a false conclusion. Perhaps voicing a worry along these lines, Kaplan complains that

Utterances take time, and utterances of distinct sentences cannot be simultaneous (i.e., in the same context). But to develop a logic of demonstratives it seems most natural to be able to evaluate several premises and a conclusion all in the same context. (Kaplan 1977: 546)

The objection returns in 'Afterthoughts':

Utterances take time, and are produced one at a time; this will not do for the analysis of validity.... even the most trivial of inferences, P therefore P, may appear invalid. (Kaplan 1989: 584)

On closer scrutiny, however, an objection of this kind is not persuasive. What it indicates is that, on the token-reflexive account, *utterances* of (1) may involve a true utterance of its premiss and a false utterance of its conclusion. Yet, this conclusion is irrelevant with respect to the logical validity of (1) and furthermore, is a result perfectly compatible with *either* of the views under discussion. A type-oriented system is by no means prevented from evaluating utterances of the premiss and conclusion in (1) in terms of distinct truth-values, as long as distinct times are at issue—that is, as long as the contexts for these utterances are represented by means of distinct indexes. However, as I explain in the next paragraphs, when it comes to the relevant relationship between the truth-values of premiss and conclusion in (1), token-reflexive approaches are by no means prevented from yielding results parallel to those obtainable on the basis of type-oriented assumptions.

On anybody's view, truth-values are assigned with respect to particular points of evaluation—in the version I am assuming for concreteness' sake, particular worlds and/or times. As explained in the previous chapters, given a sentence-type and an index, a result of unrelativized truth may be obtained within customary systems by taking into consideration the point of evaluation determined as privileged by the index—equivalently, a result of singly relativized truth-at-an-index may be derived for sentence-types alone. On the basis of results of this type, semantically interesting relationships between sentence-types may be investigated, such as the notion that, given sentences $S_1, \ldots S_n, S_{n+1}$, it is not possible that $S_1 \ldots S_n$ be mapped to the truth-value True with respect to an index i, but S_{n+1} be assigned falsehood with respect to i. Given our intuitions pertaining to the relationships between premiss and conclusion in (1), what is required is thus that, in a terminology biased in favour of a traditional approach,

> For all indexes i, if the premiss is true with respect to an index i, then the conclusion is true with respect to i.

When a requirement of this kind is rephrased in the jargon of token-reflexivity, what is desired is that, as a first approximation,

> For all indexes i, given any true token t of the premiss taking place in a context represented by i, any token t' of the conclusion taking place in that context is also true.

Trivially, any token of (a sentence-type of the form) 'I am running now' in a context turns out to be true exactly as long as any token of 'I am running now' in that context is true. Hence, the intuitively desired results regarding (1), and, more generally, pertaining to intuitively valid arguments involving multiple occurrences of indexicals, are derivable from token-reflexive treatments in as direct a manner as in more traditional views.

The issue of the validity of an argument such as (1) is closely related to questions pertaining to the peculiar status of certain sentence-types, such as

(2) I am running now iff I am running now.

Sentences such as this have an apparently interesting semantic property, one often referred to by means of connotations such as 'analytically true', 'logically true', or 'true solely in virtue of meaning'. Such a notion of logical truth, already at centre stage in Chapter 2, is also of immediate relevance to the main aim of this chapter, because it plays a central role in the argument presented in sections 3 and 4. It is thus advisable that I add a few paragraphs to the discussion of this idea, before I focus on the status of particular instances *vis-à-vis* token-reflexive theories. I then conclude this section with an explanation of why, given a development of the resources invoked in the analysis of (1), an explanation of the apparent logical truth of (2) is *not* problematic from the token-reflexive point of view. In sections 3 and 4, I proceed to the presentation of a different, less easily avoidable difficulty for token-reflexive approaches to logical truth.

As mentioned, on either token-reflexive or type-oriented views, conventional meaning 'attaches to repeatables'—that is, is a property of types. Focusing on the portion of meaning relevant for the establishment of reference or truth-value, the meaning of, say, 'now' may be presented within the terminology favoured by the traditional approach as the rule:

> The expression-type 'now' refers, with respect to any index i, to i_T.

In the token-reflexive jargon, this amounts to the claim:

> For any token t of the expression-type 'now', t refers to i_T, where i is the index representing the context in which t takes place.

Such rules yield results pertaining to 'truth in virtue of meaning' or 'logical truth'—that is, results pertaining to the special status of certain sentence-types: it is in virtue of the meaning of the expressions they involve that certain types turn out to be true at all indexes in an adequate interpretive system. For this reason, certain results of logical truth, in the sense of the term relevant here, may be compared to our intuitive assessment of the meaning of the expressions in question. For instance, a system in which, say, 'It is raining now' turns out to be true at all indexes must be unacceptable, at least with respect to our intuitive understanding of expressions such as 'now' or 'It is raining'. For if the characters it assigns to these expressions are such that the aforementioned sentence-type turns out to be logically true, it apparently must be the case that, at least for some of the expressions in question, that system's choice does not appropriately reflect their intuitive meaning. Similarly, it seems reasonable to suppose that, given what 'now', 'iff', etc. mean, a sentence-type such as (2) should indeed be evaluated as true with respect to any index whatsoever, and that analyses unable to yield this conclusion must involve hypotheses regarding these expressions' conventional profile that are empirically incorrect. What is required, in other words, is that (2) be interpreted as logically true, given an understanding of logical truth which, within the vocabulary of the customary approach, may be presented in the following terms:

> A sentence-type *s* is logically true iff it is true with respect to any index *i*.

Obviously, a result of this kind may easily be obtained when traditional type-oriented systems are applied to (2), on the basis of the usual theses pertaining to the meaning of the expressions in question.

How about token-reflexive views? Given what initially appears to be an obvious rephrasing of the foregoing requirement within its vocabulary, it would seem that what is desired in the case of (2) is a result of logical truth in the following sense of the term:

> A sentence-type *s* is logically true iff all tokens *t* of *s* are true.

Yet, one may object, this is clearly not the case: sufficiently slowly spoken utterances of (2), for instance, provide instances of tokens of (2) which are false. The strategy invoked above for the intuitive validity of (1)—namely, the imperative that different sentences be evaluated with respect to the same contextual parameters—seems idle in this case, where only one sentence is at issue.

However, this objection may easily be rebutted by means of an obvious extension of the strategy employed with respect to (1). If it is granted that commitment to tokens as bearers of semantic values does not prevent a semanticist from bracketing certain irrelevant features of the tokening process, such as the fact that spoken utterances of distinct sentences may not be simultaneous, there should be no reason why certain other accidental regularities, such as the fact that utterances often take considerable time, may not deliberately be ignored when assessing questions such as those under discussion here. Regardless of whether the utterances of the expressions in a sentence inevitably take place at distinct times, it must surely be possible to envisage the behaviour of hypothetical tokens of those expressions, given one and the same temporal instant (or, more generally, given one and the same set of parameters for the interpretation of the indexicals). If results of logical truth are obtainable within a type-oriented approach only on the basis of a definition which *guarantees* that various expressions be evaluated at one fixed index, regardless of whether they indeed are utterable in the context corresponding to that index, such a guarantee needs also to be reflected within the presentation of the requirement for logical truth within the token-reflexive framework. In general, take a sentence-type s consisting of occurrences of expression-types $e_1 \ldots e_n$ (in that order), and let v_j^i be the semantic value of a token t_j of e_j ($1 \leq j \leq n$) taking place in the context corresponding to an index i. Let V_s^i be the truth-value obtained by evaluating $e_1 \ldots e_n$ in terms of, respectively, $v_1^i \ldots v_n^i$, and by taking into consideration the compositional rules appropriate for the structure of s; then

> s is logically true iff $V_s^i =$ Truth, for any index i representing a context in which a token t_1 of e_1 takes place.

Given *this* definition, the reply to the question pertaining to the logical truth of (2) is no less trivially affirmative in a token-reflexive account than it turned out to be on the traditional analysis.

The impression that nothing of substance divides the token-reflexive approach from more traditional takes, which already emerged at the end of section 1, seems now to be reinforced. Non-reflexive type-oriented systems of the kind discussed in Chapter 1 may smoothly obtain the presumably desired results about (1) or (2) by virtue of focusing on abstract type–index pairs. Once arbitrary indexes are fixed, premiss and conclusion in (1) inevitably share their semantic profile, and, given any index i, (2) turns out to be true with respect to *i*. Of course, guarantees of this type may well be lost in the *application* of the type-theorist's apparatus to particular instances: for instance, my slow, spoken utterance of (2) may well turn out to be false, given that distinct temporal parameters may correspond to the contexts appropriate for each token of 'now'. On the other hand, token-reflexive semanticists, who develop regularities directly applicable to particular tokens, are not prevented from *abstracting* from these tokens' peculiarities, in order to discuss aspects of the conventional meaning associated with expression-types. Once this possibility is recognized, arguments that turned out to be valid in the traditional approach may also be evaluated as valid by a token-theorist, and sentences that were sanctioned as logically true in the traditional analysis may also be so classified from a token-reflexive standpoint, for parallel reasons.

The main aim of this chapter is to present an argument *against* the token-reflexive approach. Yet, the force of the argument I develop in the next two sections is most perspicuously brought to light against the background of the undeniable strengths of that approach: with certain unconvincing considerations pertaining to validity and logical truth out of the picture, the reason why token-reflexivity ultimately fails may emerge with greater clarity. In section 4, I finally explain why, notwithstanding the impression generated by these first two sections, there *are* important differences between the two approaches, which count in favour of the traditional view. Some preliminary remarks are, however, in order, pertaining to an argumentative strategy possibly suggested by Kaplan in 'Demonstratives'. I turn to its analysis in the next section.

3. The Vagaries of Action

In section 2, I rebutted on the token-reflexive theorist's behalf arguments to the effect that token-reflexivity *under*generates with respect to validity or logical truth; i.e., that it does not recognize as valid or logically true arguments and sentences which should be thus classified. In what follows, I argue that the problematic aspect in the relationships between token-reflexivity and logical truth is in fact one of *over*generation: on a token-reflexive account, certain non-logically-true sentences turn out to be logical truths.

The point is most perspicuously introduced by focusing on the comment which, in 'Afterthoughts', Kaplan appends to the aforementioned remarks about the time it takes to produce an utterance. He writes:

there are sentences which express a truth in certain contexts, but not if uttered. For example, 'I say nothing'. Logic and semantics are concerned not with the vagaries of actions, but with the verities of meanings. (Kaplan 1989: 584–5)

Correctly perceiving that the objection is directed, perhaps among other things, against a token-reflexive approach, Garcia-Carpintero responds to what he calls a 'subsidiary, minor argument' for type-oriented views along the following lines:

What exactly is the argument? It cannot be that we, as ordinary speakers, have the intuition, which any correct theory should honour, that the 'sentence-in-context' at stake is true: for there is no such intuition... Where are the pressing linguistic data to be accounted by this? (Garcia-Carpintero 1998: 547)

Kaplan's commentary is brief, and the scholarly question of whether Garcia-Carpintero's reply addresses the point Kaplan had in mind is not immediately relevant for my purpose here. What is important is that, at least on a certain reading of Kaplan's objection, the question at issue is not one directly pertaining to the intuitively correct truth-values of certain sentences (clauses) with respect to (the indexes representing) particular contexts—or, if you prefer, pertaining to the truth-values of certain

90 ~ *The Vagaries of Action*

clause–index pairs. The point that Kaplan is apparently raising does not consist in the tenet that, given a particular context *c*, sentences such as 'I say nothing' ought to be evaluated as true with respect to (the index representing) *c* because, given that very context and that sentence, we intuitively require a verdict of this kind. The point is, rather, the existentially generalized claim that *there is* at least an index with respect to which 'I say nothing' should come out true—a claim that is not grounded on presumed intuitions regarding the truth-value of one particular instance or another. Kaplan's brief remark does not spell out the reason for subscribing to such an existential generalization, but the position of the passage I just cited provides important indications in this respect: Kaplan's comment on 'I say nothing' occurs immediately after the complaint discussed in section 2 regarding the token-reflexive theorist's presumed inability to deal with the validity of arguments such as (1) or the logical truth of certain sentences. As I explained, when it comes to cases such as (1), token-reflexive approaches do not appear to be in the uncomfortable position depicted by Kaplan. What are important at this stage, however, are not Kaplan's views about cases involving multiple tokenings of 'now'. What matters is, rather, the indirect indication that what may be at issue with respect to, for instance, 'I say nothing' are considerations of logical truth—that is, issues pertaining to the intuitive *meaning* of the expressions involved in such examples.

Given this argumentative line, Garcia-Carpintero's objection that we lack firm intuitions regarding the truth of 'I say nothing' with respect to certain particular contexts appears irrelevant. What is relevant, on the other hand, is whether the argumentative strategy that may emerge from the foregoing reading of Kaplan's remark is indeed convincing against token-reflexive views. In this section, I present the argument in question by focusing on Kaplan-inspired examples, I explain why it is compelling against traditional versions of token-reflexivity, but

I conclude that it is *not* a conclusive reasoning against token-reflexivity *per se*. In section 4, I argue that a more suitable development of the strategy in question may indeed provide a convincing argument against token-reflexivity.

For simplicity's sake, I focus here on the positive counterpart of Kaplan's suggestion: namely, the question of whether 'I say something' should turn out false at some index. I also substitute 'say' by 'utter', in a sense of the word neutral with respect to the non-immediately relevant distinction between events involving speaking, writing, flashing on a screen, etc. Consider then:

(3) I am uttering something now,

together with the closely related case of

(4) A token exists now.[3]

When spelled out in some detail, the Kaplan-inspired argument against token-reflexivity involves two premisses:

(a) Given competent speakers' intuitions regarding the meaning of the expressions in (3) and (4), these sentences should not turn out to be logically true.

And

(b) It is a consequence of token-reflexive approaches that they are logically true.

The conclusion, of course, is that token-reflexive views yield inadequate results of 'truth in virtue of meaning'. In the following paragraphs, I begin with a defence of (a); I then turn to an explanation of why premiss (b), though correct with respect to typical versions of token-reflexivity, is not true *in general*.

---

[3] More appropriately, 'a tokening event occurs now' and 'a token-object is being tokened now'; the distinction between the occurrence of an event and the existence of an object, though important in its own right, does not play a crucial role in the arguments in this essay.

Only a few, easily eliminable confusions are responsible for doubts regarding (a), when it comes to cases such as (3) or (4). Clearly, what matters for our understanding of 'I' or 'now'—that is, what is encoded in the meaning conventionally associated with these expressions—is the notion that the former refers to a certain individual, and the latter refers to a certain time, independently of the existence of acts of utterance. It is true that, informally, the system's rule for, say, 'now', is often presented with the aid of descriptions such as 'the time of utterance'. But informal statements of this type are nothing more than useful rules of thumb, which conjoin two importantly different regularities: on the one hand, the conventional rule steering the behaviour of 'now'— namely, the rule that it refers to the contextually salient time— and on the other hand, the relatively reliable suggestion that, more often than not, a certain time is rendered appropriately salient by virtue of the occurrence of an utterance. Similar considerations hold *mutatis mutandis* for 'I', and, of course, for nonindexical expressions such as 'something' or 'utter': there are no more reasons for supposing that, once 'utter' is being evaluated at an index i, there exist utterances in i_W, than for supposing that, say, for any index i at which 'tiger' is interpreted, large striped cats must populate its world. It follows that nothing in the meaning of the expressions occurring in (3) or (4) *guarantees* that, given any index i, the system ought to evaluate them as true with respect to i: for nothing in these expressions' meaning requires that, at the possible world i_W, i_A is indeed uttering something at time i_T, and that a token is indeed present at that time, in that world.

In other words, suppose that, as alleged by the aforementioned rule of thumb, uses of 'now' refer to the time of speaking, so that, given an utterance of a sentence containing 'now', the index representing the context of utterance includes a possible world i_W in which an act of tokening takes place. Suppose, then, that utterances of, say, (4) turn out true; that is, that (4) is true with respect to all indexes representing contexts in which its utterances take place. Still, a presumed regularity of this kind is irrelevant with respect to issues of logical truth—that is, truth in virtue of meaning—as long as it is not encoded in the very meaning of the expressions in question. What the meaning of, for instance, 'now' guarantees is that a certain contextually salient time is being selected; whether such a time is, more or less inevitably, a time of speaking is at best an inescapable feature of how temporal instants are raised to salience. This independently plausible conclusion may of course be conclusively reinforced by the considerations from Chapter 2, to the effect that expressions such as 'now' or 'I' may actually be *used* so as to refer to a time at which no tokening takes place, or to an individual who is not performing the utterance in question. For if this is indeed the case, the 'rule of thumb' in question is not only irrelevant to the establishment of logical truth, but also straightforwardly false: that at i_T, the time selected by 'now', someone is uttering something in i_W turns out to be not even an inevitable effect of the mechanisms affecting contextual salience, let alone a consequence of any expression's meaning.

Let us take stock. When it comes to cases such as (3) and (4), I explained why, even if it were the case that all utterances of these sentences turned out to be true, such a result should not be interpreted as evidence of logical truth: their presumed truth would be the outcome of regularities that are not encoded within the meaning of the expressions in question—i.e., regularities that are not reflected within the interpretive system. The examples in Chapter 2 provide *additional* evidence for this conclusion: 'now' or 'I' may actually be used in order to refer to items other than the time of utterance or the speaker. But it should be stressed that my treatment of the examples in Chapter 2 is by no means *necessary* for this section's main argument, as presented above: even those who disagree with my analysis of, say, 'I am not here now' ought to concede the initial plausibility of premiss (a), according to which the parameters of utterance are not inevitably addressed by virtue of the *meaning* of the indexicals in question. In other words, even if, contrary to the evidence from Chapter 2, 'now' and 'I' were always employed so as to refer to the time of utterance and the utterer, such a conclusion would by no means suffice for the surprising claim that the conventional meaning of, say, 'now' includes reference to an act of tokening. Even more importantly, my hypotheses regarding the particular examples (3) and (4), be they grounded on the considerations of Chapter 2 or on independent motives, are not ultimately essential for the main argument presented in the next section, and are intended only as important preliminaries to the central case against token-reflexivity. For, as I explained a few paragraphs ago, the Kaplan-inspired argument grounded on (3) or (4) is ultimately insufficient, and needs to be revised; yet, when it comes to the more satisfactory version which will be presented in section 4, the claim parallel to premiss (a) turns out to be even less objectionable than the already plausible hypothesis that (3) and (4) should not turn out to be logically true.

What remains to be assessed in the Kaplan-inspired argument discussed in this section is premiss (b): namely, the claim that token-reflexive accounts inevitably render (3) or (4) logically true. In the next paragraphs I explain why token-reflexive theorists may resist a conclusion of this type; in section 4, I present a different version of the argument, one that may not be rebutted as easily by defenders of the token-reflexive approach.

Consider presentations of token-reflexive rules for, say, 'now' or 'I', as in:

> For any token t of 'now', t refers to the time when t was spoken.

Or

> For any token t of 'I', the referent of t is the speaker who has uttered t.

According to this approach, reference to an act of utterance is part and parcel of the conventional rules steering the semantic behaviour of indexical expressions. When such rules are expressed within the vocabulary I suggested in this paper, they amount to the conjunction of the claim that

> for any token t of 'now', t refers to i_T, where i is the index representing the context in which t takes place,

or

> for any token t of 'I', t refers to i_A, where i is the index representing the context in which t takes place,

together with the further tenet that

> (∗) for any index i appropriate to the representation of a context of tokening, i is such that i_A is uttering something at i_T in i_W.

It follows on this view that, given any index i of the type appropriate to the semantic evaluation of an indexical language (i.e., according to the foregoing rules, any index representing a context in which a token takes place), the referent i_A of 'I' is uttering something at the time i_T referred to by 'now', and hence *a fortiori* that an act of utterance does indeed exist at that time in the index's possible world i_W. Hence, it is a consequence of this stance that, for any semantically relevant index, (3) and (4) are true; i.e., that they are logical truths.

Premiss (b) is thus undoubtedly correct with respect to the rules most frequently proposed by token-reflexive theorists, and a convincing argument can thus be mounted against such a presentation of token-reflexivity. What is important for the purpose of this essay, however, is not this weaker conclusion, but rather the stronger claim that token-reflexivity *per se* yields such undesirable results. Nevertheless, this stronger thesis is by no means as straightforwardly obtainable as the foregoing criticism of particular versions of token-reflexive treatments of indexicality, especially if one takes into account the remarks proposed on behalf of the token-reflexive approach in section 2. There, I developed a neutral version of the token-reflexive approach, one that deliberately avoided endorsing the identification of the contextually appropriate agent or time as the speaker or the time of utterance—that is, I refrained from burdening the token-reflexive approach with additional assumptions of representation along the lines of (∗). Given a statement such as, for instance,

> for any token t of 'now', the referent of t is i_T, where i is the index representing the context in which t takes place,

it seems perfectly consistent with a token-reflexive approach to insist that, although it may *perhaps* be the case that i_T is inevitably a time of speaking, such additional information may not be recognized as a restriction on the class of indexes which the interpretive system may take into consideration, but at best only as an unavoidable regularity affecting the situations in which certain expressions are used. Token-reflexive theorists willing to accept my analysis of the examples in Chapter 2 may in fact go as far as denying the inevitability of such presumed regularity altogether. For instance, they may agree that, in the context for some tokens of 'now', what is salient is not the time at which those tokens take place, but rather, say, a time intended as relevant by the speaker, or something along these lines. It follows from this view not only that systems ought to consider indexes i such that i_A is not uttering anything at i_T in i_W, but also that indexes of this type may indeed be involved in the representation of actual instances of language use. Once indexes of this kind are admitted within the system—i.e., are taken as relevant to the assessment of validity—sentences such as (3) and (4) are correctly expelled from the realm of logical truths.

Thus, although (3) and (4) may well be problematic for traditional versions of token-reflexivity, in that they are incorrectly evaluated as logically true, such undesirable results are obtainable only on the basis of additional assumptions such as (∗), which are, strictly speaking, independent of the token-reflexive standpoint. This conclusion nevertheless does not suffice as a conclusive defence of token-reflexivity: as I explain in the next section, the argumentative structure developed thus far may be reformulated by focusing on other, more appropriate examples, thereby providing important considerations in favour of traditional, non-reflexive treatments of indexicality.

4. Refining the Case against Token-Reflexivity

Although Kaplan's example 'I say nothing' and the related cases of (3) and (4) do not provide the evidence needed for a convincing counter-argument against token-reflexivity, the following sentences suggest a more persuasive version of the reasoning in section 3:

(5) Either a token exists now, or it has existed in the past, or will exist in the future.

And

(6) Something either exists now, has existed, or will exist.

The defence of premiss (a) with respect to these examples is straightforward, given the foregoing considerations regarding 'now' and other expressions: on pretty much nobody's view, for instance, do expressions such as 'something' or 'exist' require, in virtue of their very meaning, that tokens of 'something', of 'exist', or for that matter of any other expression do indeed take place.

However, (6) deserves a brief parenthetical comment, before I continue with the presentation of the argument against token-reflexivity. The customary counterpart of a sentence such as (6) (or at least of its presentation by means of a tenseless predicate 'there exist something') within the standard, indexical-free language of first-order logic with identity—namely, something along the lines of $\exists x \exists y (x = y)$—is classically interpreted as logically true, in virtue of the explicit prohibition of an empty universe: since, by stipulation, no model is associated with the empty set, it follows that a sentence to the effect that something exists is inevitably evaluated as true. The discussion of the function and legitimacy of such an important stipulation in the model-theoretic treatment of formal languages is not of immediate relevance to my topic in this essay. What matters is, rather, the analysis of the status of (6) with respect to the logical treatment of indexical languages, *independently* of issues pertaining to the correctness of the stipulation in question. At least on the assumption of what Kaplan calls 'the neotraditional logic that countenances empty worlds' (Kaplan 1977: 549), if the foregoing remarks about meaning are on the right track, then (6) should *not* turn out to be logically true (*pace* Kaplan's claim to the contrary, discussed in Chapter 2): nothing in the *meaning* of 'something' or 'exists' is such that it guarantees the existence of something, in the manner required for a conclusion of logical truth. That is to say, nothing (at most with the exception of stipulations *additional* to the information encoded at the level of meaning) ensures that, given any index i for the evaluation of (6), i_W is non-empty, and hence that (6) should turn out true with respect to i.

What remains to be discussed is a version of premiss (b) above focused on cases such as (5) and (6): namely, the tenet that token-reflexive theories inevitably yield incorrect results of logical truth for such sentences. As explained in the previous sections, a version of token-reflexivity may be developed which is able to provide an analysis of meaning in abstraction from the presumed features of the tokening process, such as the accidental facts that, at least more often than not, the context's agent is speaking and that the utterance of an argument requires a non-insignificant

The Vagaries of Action ~ 99

temporal interval. It is also the case, however, that, when it comes to questions such as the assignment of reference or truth-value, token-reflexivity is inevitably committed to a reflexive account in terms of tokens: expression-tokens refer, and sentence-tokens are assigned a truth-value, according to the regularities sanctioned by reflexive rules. Such a reflexive appeal to tokens is inevitably reflected within the theory's understanding of interpretive systems, in particular with respect to the assignment of reference to simple indexicals. For instance, what the meaning of 'now' allegedly tells us, according to the token-reflexive theorist's understanding of that expression's character, is that, given any index *representing a context involving a token t* of 'now', *t* refers to a certain item with respect to that index.

If the regularities encoded in an expression's meaning sanction its behaviour only with respect to indexes of this type, what is required by a definition of 'truth in virtue of meaning alone' is a verdict of truth not at all indexes whatsoever, but only at all indexes *representing a context of tokening*. In other words, the indexes that interpretive systems are allowed to consider, according to the token-reflexive approach, are only indexes of this kind. Indeed, as emerged from the discussion in section 2, logical truth is defined within the token-reflexive vocabulary along the following lines (leaving aside, for simplicity's sake, the complications related to instances involving multiple occurrences of an indexical):

> A sentence-type *s* is logically true iff *s* is true on an interpretation of the expressions in *s* with respect to an index *i*, for any index *i* representing a context in which a token *t* of *s* takes place.

In other words, if the very meaning of, say, 'now' is encoded by means of a rule that addresses its semantic behaviour only at those indexes that correspond to contexts of tokening, the notion of 'truth in virtue of meaning' is inevitably cashed out in terms of truth at all indexes *of that kind*. Yet, the class of such indexes is a proper subclass of the class of all indexes: in the possible world i_W determined by an index representing a context of tokening, a token has taken place, either at i_T or at some other time. This restriction is obviously less dramatic than that proposed by (*) in section 3: for instance, as we have seen, it is consistent with a token-oriented approach that certain contexts be represented by means of indexes i, such that i_T, the contextually salient time, is not the time of utterance. To put it otherwise, it is consistent with, say, the token-reflexive rule of meaning for 'now' that the class of semantically relevant indexes includes n-tuples i such that in i_W the individual i_A is not uttering anything at i_T, and such that no token at all is present at that time. Still, one important restriction remains in place: n-tuples $<i_A, i_L, i_T, i_W>$ may not qualify as indexes—i.e., as collections of the parameters required by the indexicals' characters—if no token has ever occurred in i_W.

The restriction of the class of parameters relevant to the assessment of logical truth inevitably yields results that are not obtainable with respect to an unrestricted definition. Sentences (5) and (6) are indeed among the central examples of sentences true with respect to any index corresponding to a context of tokening, but not true with respect to all indexes whatsoever. Once this result is conjoined with premiss (a)—namely, the claim that (5) and (6) do not deserve the status of logical truth—it follows that the token-reflexive approach overgenerates with respect to logical truth. By virtue of presenting the rules steering the semantic profile of the expressions in the language in terms of the behaviour of tokens of those expressions, token-reflexivity is inevitably committed to an analysis restricted to a particular subclass of the parameters required for the interpretation of indexicals. This class is a proper subclass of the set of all indexes, because contexts of tokening are inevitably structured affairs: the very metaphysics of the act of tokening, such as the facts that a token does indeed take place or that no tokening may occur in an empty world, illegitimately constrains semantic evaluation on the basis of the (more or less ontologically inevitable, yet unquestionably semantically accidental) 'vagaries of action'.

5. The Vagaries Strike Back

In section 4, I proposed an argument against token-reflexivity alternative to certain considerations put forth by the defenders of the traditional approach. In attempting to identify the most appropriate premises involved in a persuasive attack on token-reflexive accounts of indexicality, I distinguished between the essential traits of token-reflexivity and some widespread, but independent assumptions with which it is often conjoined. This distinction is of interest independently of the assessment of token-reflexivity: if certain undesirable claims regarding the structure and make-up of contexts may be taken for granted regardless of one's stance with respect to the type–token dispute, it is at least possible in theory that they also vitiate approaches of a more traditional, type-oriented type.

In fact, as I pointed out in Chapter 2, this turns out to be more than a mere conceptual possibility: customary versions of the type-oriented orthodoxy, not unlike their token-reflexive alternatives, more or less explicitly entangle the evaluation of indexical languages with independent, extraneous claims pertaining to the structure of the indexes admitted within the interpretive system. The case of Kaplan's 'Demonstratives' is particularly instructive in this respect. As his choice of 'I say nothing' as a counter-example to token-reflexivity indirectly indicates, Kaplan (correctly) denies relevance to *some* presumed regularities affecting the process of utterance: in particular, the notion that the referent for 'I' must be uttering something at the time selected by 'now'. More formally, the system of 'Demonstratives' is devised so as to take into consideration indexes i, such that i_A is *not* uttering anything at i_T in i_W. However, as discussed in Chapter 2, the class of admissible indexes is explicitly restricted to a proper subclass of indexes along alternative lines—that is, in terms of what is customarily called a 'proper' index. Not unlike the notion that i_A is uttering something at i_T, or that a token exists at i_W, the denial of semantic relevance to improper indexes may not be derived as a consequence of any rule establishing the conventional profile of indexical expressions, but must be presupposed by *fiat*, within the clauses defining the structure of Kaplan's model-theoretic apparatus. Given that the class of proper indexes is a proper subclass of the class of all indexes, sentences whose conventional profile does not guarantee results of logical truth are nevertheless evaluated as logically true. The list of undesirable inclusions, as I pointed out in Chapter 2, includes 'I am here now' and 'I exist'.

Kaplan's label of *contexts* for what I call 'indexes' may well be at the root of such infelicitous restrictions: the very definition of the sequence of parameters relevant to the interpretation of indexicals—that is, the definition of 'context' in the technical sense of the term—is marred by connotations typical of the everyday employment of 'context', roughly as the (alleged) type of situation in which an utterance takes place. An equivocation of this type becomes explicit in Kaplan's later commentary on logical truth, in which the notion of 'context' is blatantly analysed in terms of context *of use*:

Any feature of a possible world which flows from the fact that it contains the context of use may yield validity without necessity.... not every possible circumstance of evaluation is associated with an (appropriate) possible context of use, in other words, not every possible-world is a possible actual-world. Though there may be circumstances in which no one exists, no possible context of use can occur in such circumstances. (Kaplan 1989: 596–7)

Given that some of my considerations regarding the meaning of indexical expressions are also applicable to the classic framework provided by Kaplan's 'Demonstratives', it may be objected that my attack on token-reflexivity also ends up affecting type-oriented approaches: what my argument achieves is, on this view, a hollow victory, given that both parties in the token–type dispute end up being in the wrong. However, the particular features peculiar to certain versions of the token-reflexive and the traditional views are not my primary target here. For instance, regarding token-reflexivity, I explained in section 3 why customary presentations of this standpoint err in presenting the meaning of indexicals by appealing to presumed regularities affecting all instances of speaking (or, more generally, uttering). But I also explicitly stressed that this additional feature is not essential to the token-reflexive stance *per se*, and that the problematic consequences it entails are not by themselves sufficient as counter-arguments to token-reflexivity. Similarly, Kaplan's take on 'I am here now' or 'Something exists' and his accompanying views on contexts, though affected by some of the considerations I employed against token-reflexivity, are by no means essential to the structure of the traditional view. What is important from the point of view of this essay is not the decision pertaining to particular versions of one approach or another, but rather the extent to which either treatment of indexicality may be developed in a manner consistent with the correct assessment of logical truth, i.e., truth in virtue of meaning. In this sense, regardless of the idiosyncrasies of famous versions of either approach, the type-oriented view is clearly preferable: token-reflexivity is *committed* to incorrect logical results, whereas customary non-reflexive, type-oriented analyses are not.

6. More Vagaries

In Chapter 2 and in the previous sections of this chapter, I have discussed a variety of examples in which *presumed* warranted utterability (i.e., the alleged fact that certain sentences may always be uttered truly) does not correspond to a result of truth in virtue of meaning. Thus, even if it were the case that, contrary to some of the considerations in Chapter 2, all utterances end up being represented by means of a simple-minded index, 'I am here now' would not thereby qualify as a logical truth within the interpretive system: the accidental alleged regularity pertaining to the structure of contexts of utterance would still not be encoded within the meaning of the expressions in question. Additional evidence for this conclusion is of course provided by counter-examples to the 'regularity' in question: for instance, if 'I' is actually employed, according to its customary meaning, so as to refer to someone other than the speaker, it must surely be the case that its ability to refer to the speaker is not an immediate consequence of its conventional profile. My discussion of the relationships between meaning and truth, on the one hand, and certain supposed generalizations about utterances, on the other, turned out to be of use also in this chapter, where I discussed the limits of the token-reflexive approach. Regardless of whether utterances of those sentences turn out inevitably to be true, cases such as (5) and (6) should not be evaluated as logically true.

The relationship between meaning, truth, and the use of language is the central topic of this essay. As I explained, certain presumed regularities affecting typical utterances may not inevitably be translated into conclusions pertaining to meaning, and to its relationship with matters of truth-value. Traditional interpretive systems, with their attention to abstract items such as clause–index pairs, turn out to be a remarkably efficient tool in the investigation of these matters. In the final section of this chapter, I present some additional considerations in this vein, having to do with a variety of cases quite distinct from those I have discussed thus far. The issue on which I now focus is, in a sense, complementary to the phenomenon of (allegedly) warrantedly true utterances that do not qualify as logically true: what I now focus on are examples that do qualify as logically true, but which may in fact be uttered falsely. Similarly, I consider logically equivalent sentences S_1 and S_2 whose utterances differ in truth-value, and utterances of sentences S_3 and S_4 that are respectively true and false, notwithstanding the fact that S_3 entails S_4. Incidentally, a couple of independent considerations I employ in what follows will also be of use later in the book, in particular in Chapter 5.

A good starting example is the relatively straightforward Quine-inspired case of

> (7) If Giorgione was so-called because of his size, and if Giorgione is Barbarelli, then Barbarelli was so-called because of his size.[4]

Since Barbarelli was indeed called 'Giorgione' in virtue of his size, and since Giorgione is none other than Barbarelli, the antecedent in (7) is apparently true. Its consequent seems, however, not to be truly utterable: nothing in the name 'Barbarelli' gives any indication regarding its bearer's dimensions. It follows that typical utterances of (7) are false. Still, (7) arguably expresses a logical truth. In particular, at least according to a prima-facie eminently plausible analysis, the names 'Giorgione' and 'Barbarelli' occur in what is often called a transparent position: they do not, for instance, occur within quotation marks or other operators of this kind. And occurrences of proper names in such positions are apparently amenable to a process of substitution of co-referential expressions, so that (7) is logically equivalent to the trivial 'If Giorgione was so-called because of its size, and if Giorgione is Giorgione, then Giorgione was so-called because of its size.'

---

[4] See Quine 1960; see also Crimmins 1992b; Forbes 1990; Salmon 1995.

I called this example 'straightforward' because the analysis of the predicament summarized in the foregoing paragraph is not particularly puzzling. The first conjunct in the antecedent of (7) and its consequent contain occurrences of a demonstrative expression, 'so': to be so-called means to be called *that*. Words, not unlike other kinds of individuals, are possible targets for demonstrative expressions: for instance, I may point to a token of 'rhinoceros' in a book and say 'That is a difficult word to spell'. Overt acts of ostension are not always necessary; in certain cases, the *use* of an expression typically contributes to rendering it contextually salient, thereby constituting an available target for successive occurrences of demonstrative expressions. So, if you say 'There are fewer rhinoceroses these days', I may comment 'That is a difficult word to spell', and thereby refer to one among the expressions you just used. It is in this manner that the demonstrative 'so' in the first part of (7) typically manages to obtain its reference: by virtue of using 'Giorgione', utterances of 'Giorgione was so-called because of its size' normally generate a context in which the name 'Giorgione' is suitably salient. Contexts of this kind, of course, are representable within the interpretive system by means of indexes in which the expression 'Giorgione' occurs as the *demonstratum* parameter. Typical utterances of the sentence in the consequent, on the other hand, are responsible for raising to contextual salience another appellation of the Italian painter, thereby providing a different *demonstratum* as the target for 'so'. It follows that utterances of this type are evaluated correctly by taking into consideration an index different from that appropriate for typical utterances of the first part of (7). For this reason, the (correct) notion that utterances of the antecedent, unlike utterances of the consequent, appear to be true, and the resultant conclusion that utterances of (7) may be false, has no bearing on matters of logical truth—that is, on questions pertaining to the truth-value of (7) *vis-à-vis* all indexes, as long as all the indexicals occurring in that sentence are

The Vagaries of Action ~ 107

simultaneously interpreted with respect to one and the same index.[5]

Since a couple of relatively uncontroversial assumptions embedded in the foregoing paragraphs will turn out to be of use for the otherwise quite different problem discussed in Chapter 5, it is fitting that I highlight them at this stage and label them for further reference. Let me, then, employ the expression *Verbal Salience Thesis* for the claim that

> Utterances of an expression e in a suitable context c may contribute to rendering e salient in c in such a manner that e may occur as the *demonstratum* parameter in the index appropriately representing c.

The Verbal Salience Thesis may, however, remain on the back burner for a while, and plays no immediate role in my analysis of the examples in the following paragraphs.

The conclusion about (7) reached thus far is the quite unsurprising notion that utterances of logically true sentences may turn out to be false, as long the indexicals or demonstratives they involve get interpreted *vis-à-vis* distinct indexes. Interestingly, however, such a condition pertaining to the evaluation of indexical expressions is not a *necessary* condition for the discrepancy between logical properties and the truth-values of the utterances in question. In the remainder of this section, I consider two interesting issues, pertaining respectively to the so-called puzzle of addressing and to certain cases involving approximations. My conclusions are parallel to those reached with respect to the case of (7). In particular, I consider pairs of sentences that are logically equivalent (i.e., that are such that appropriate systems evaluate

---

[5] It may be worth noting that, although *typical* utterances of (7) inevitably end up involving a true utterance of the antecedent and a false utterance of the consequent, that is by no means *always* the case. Suppose we are contemplating a large sign with 'Giorgione' written on it. Pointing to the sign, I utter (7). My utterance is now apparently true: Barbarelli was indeed called *that*—namely, 'Giorgione'—because of his size.

the biconditional containing them as logically true). I then explain why the scenarios in which one may be uttered truly but the other may not inevitably involve cases of 'index shifting' irrelevant to the definition of validity. But, the analysis of these examples also sheds further light on the role which indexes play within interpretive systems for indexical languages: the contrasting utterances of the sentences in question may well be assumed to take place within contexts representable by indexes that provide the *same* interpretation to the indexical expression they contain.

The 'puzzle of addressing'[6] has to do with the meaning and use of honorifics and similar expressions—for example, the use of 'Sie' instead of the more familiar 'du' in German, or the use of the formal 'Lei' instead of 'tu' in Italian. In order to avoid burdening this essay with examples involving foreign languages, I shall reproduce this distinction by means of the quasi-English expression 'you$_{form}$' and 'you$_{inf}$', alluding to, respectively, a formal and informal version of the second person singular pronoun. The puzzle of addressing may be introduced by focusing on the following pair of sentences:

(8) I never address you$_{inf}$ formally

and

(9) I never address you$_{form}$ formally.

Clearly, (8) may be employed as a true comment on the speaker's familiarity with a certain addressee a, but (9) is apparently always uttered falsely, regardless of whether it is directed towards a or anybody else: the very utterance of (9) provides counter-evidence against the claim that the addressee is never spoken to in a formal manner. Of course, the truth-values of the utterances under

---

[6] Zimmermann 1997 calls it the 'addressing puzzle'; see also Tsohatzidis 1992.

discussion may be obtained without shifting the interpretation of the indexical expressions 'you$_{inf}$' and 'you$_{form}$'. Fix any time, agent, addressee, or location: utterances of (8) and (9) still differ in truth-value. Yet (8) and (9) are arguably logically equivalent: with respect to any index, they share their unrelativized truth-value within the system. For it appears that, given any index i, both second person pronouns refer to the addressee of i, and hence that both are true iff that individual is never being formally addressed by i_A, the agent of i.

This situation is puzzling only on the erroneous assumption that questions pertaining to the identification of a particular index have to do solely with the interpretation of indexical expressions. It is true that it is perfectly possible to envision true utterances of (8) and false utterances of (9) taking place in contexts that supply the same items to the interpretation of the verb's tense or the personal pronouns. It does not follow, however, that these utterances are appropriately representable by means of one and the same index: although the indexes with respect to which (8) turns out to be true may well agree in their agent, temporal, or addressee parameters with the indexes at which (9) is evaluated as false, this agreement does not amount to what is required for a befuddling clash with the notion that (8) and (9) are logically equivalent. Recall in particular that, as I explained in Chapter 1, indexes serve a double purpose within traditional interpretive systems: they not only provide the coordinates required by the meaning of indexical expressions; they also supply the point of evaluation appropriate to the establishment of unrelativized truth-value. Given an index containing myself and 15 October, a sentence such as

(10) I am hungry now

turns out to be true at certain points of evaluation, false at others; but the sentence index in question is evaluated as true *tout court* iff it is true at the point determined by the index. It follows that, given two indexes i_1 and i_2 that agree in their agent and temporal co-ordinates—that is, that agree with respect to the interpretation of the indexicals in (10)—(10) may nevertheless be true with respect to i_1, but false with respect to i_2: the worlds they determine may after all differ precisely with respect to my appetite on that day.

Let us then return to (8) and (9). Given one and the same index, the sentences in (8) and (9) must unquestionably share their truth-value within the interpretive system. Still, *uttering* (9) may well change the way things happen to be with respect to the subject-matter under discussion—namely, the speaker's use of deferential forms of address. By virtue of my employment of 'you$_{form}$', the situation in which my utterance takes place is one in which, indeed, I occasionally address you formally. In the jargon I opted for, the index i appropriate to the context of an utterance of (9) is such that at i_W, its world co-ordinate, the speaker does at least once employ an honorific in addressing her audience. With respect to indexes of *this* type, however, (8) turns out to be untrue as well. Consider, on the other hand, any index i appropriate to true utterances of (8). In this case, i must include a world i_W such that, in i_W, the speaker never employs the formal pronoun in her conversation with the addressee. With respect to this index, of course, (9) is also evaluated as true, regardless of the fact that no utterance of (9) may possibly be representable by virtue of it.

Similar considerations may be applied to a prima-facie unrelated type of example, yet one equally instructive for an appreciation of the roles played by indexes within the system: namely, examples involving expressions of measurement and what may be called 'approximate uses'. Consider the following sentences:

(11) This table is 120 cm long.
(12) This table is more than 119.999 cm long.

Granting certain obvious implicit assumptions (say, that 120 is larger than 119.999 and that if an object is n cm long, then it is more than m cm long, whenever $n > m$), (11) entails (12): for any index i, if (11) is true with respect to i, so is (12). Yet, as I explain in what follows, there exist situations in which an utterance of (11) is apparently true, but an utterance of (12) is not.

Consider my use of (11) during a discussion in a furniture store. My utterance seems intuitively true even in a situation in which, when measured with techniques borrowed from experimental physics, the table's length turns out to be exactly 119.998 cm. Since 119.998 is not the same as 120, two alternative explanations of our prima-facie evaluation of my utterance may be proposed initially. According to the first, my utterance is actually false, notwithstanding competent speakers' willingness to accept it as true. According to the other explanation, my utterance is true, but only because it is *short for* an utterance of 'This table is approximately 120 cm long'. Although I shall not attempt to provide counter-arguments to either of these suggestions, their prima-facie unpalatability ought to encourage unbiased semanticists to search for analyses along alternative lines. As for the first proposal, it seems at least uncomfortable to conclude that, on ordinary occasions, we almost never correctly assess an object's size or weight, the distance between two points, or the duration of a certain interval, even in cases in which the presumably correct description would easily be at our disposal. It is at least odd to suppose that, say, Jones's physician utters falsehoods when she reports that her patient is 173 cm tall, rather than the more adequate 173.2 cm: for her interest in providing a true report ought to be a sufficient incentive for the minimal additional effort required in uttering either 'more or less' or 'and two millimetres'. As for the other suggestion, it is questionable that a methodologically satisfactory sense of 'short for' may be found, according to which an utterance of (11) is indeed short for an utterance of 'This table is approximately 120 cm long'. There is, of course, a weak understanding of the relationship between (11) and the parallel sentence containing 'approximately': at least in some scenarios, utterances of the former ought to be associated with a semantic profile identical to that for utterances of the latter. A proposal of this kind, however, is not an *explanation* of the semantic profile of the utterances in question, but merely a statement of the *explanandum*.

Suppose, then, that my utterance of (11) is indeed true in the scenario under discussion. But imagine that, overhearing my remark, you add:

(12) This table is more than 119.999 cm long.

At least, continuing to take for granted the reliability of our intuitions in this respect, it seems unlikely that we would be right in accepting your remark, simply on the basis of the fact that we all agreed with my utterance of (11). The typical (and correct) reaction to a comment such as (12) is rather something along the lines of

Well, if you want to be so precise, no, the table isn't more than 119.999 cm long, it is actually only 119.998 cm long.

If these initial inclinations are on the right track, it follows that my utterance of (11) is true, and that your utterance of (12) is false, even though the table did not shrink or expand in the time separating your rejoinder from my commentary.

A thorough defence of the foregoing assessment of the truth-values of the utterances in question goes beyond the limits of this section. What is more immediately relevant for my purpose is rather the weaker claim that, even assuming that such an assessment is indeed correct, the discrepancy in truth-values between utterances of (11) and (12) is no counter-example to the logical thesis put forth a couple of paragraphs ago, to the effect that (11) entails (12). As was the case with (8) and (9), though, insistence that all indexicals be interpreted with respect to identical parameters does not seem to be of particular relevance at this stage. The only indexicals involved in (11) and (12) are the demonstrative

The Vagaries of Action ~ 113

expression 'this table' and the verb's present tense, and both my utterance and your reply address one and the same *demonstratum*, and take place at times which, for all relevant purposes, may be supposed to be simultaneous. Still, as I argue in what follows, a type of 'index shifting' similar to that invoked in my analysis of (8) and (9) is also at work in the cases under analysis.

Consider the following rough picture of the type of measuring practices appropriate on different occasions. For the purposes relevant in everyday situations, the dimensions of objects such as tables or chairs are assessed by comparing the object's extension with a measuring-rod marked at, say, half-centimetre intervals: on such occasions, what is required for the truth of an utterance of 'a is n cm long' is that, when one extreme of a coincides with the measuring-rod's initial mark, the other extreme coincides with a point on the rod included between n and $(n - 0.5\,\text{cm})$.[7] On other occasions, such as the demanding situations common for the purpose of scientific measurement, the practice of the assessment of an object's length involves rods gauged at finer intervals, say, one-hundredth of a millimetre: an utterance of 'a is n cm long' counts as true on such occasions iff a's extremity fits within the interval between n and $(n - 0.001\,\text{cm})$. The setting at the furniture store is, initially, an obvious example of what I called an 'everyday' scenario: given the purpose relevant on that occasion, descriptions sensitive to practically invisible discriminations are merely distracting. In such a setting, then, my utterance of (11) is true: the table fits the extremes within the measuring-scale appropriate for the case at hand. Your utterance of (12), however, is responsible for an important contextual shift: by virtue of employing expressions such as '119.999 cm', the speaker

---

[7] The details of this sketchy picture are of course not immediately relevant. For instance, nothing in what follows depends on the choice of 0.5 cm as the interval appropriate in everyday situations; similarly, that the interval in question is in all likelihood only vaguely determined is compatible with the proposal in the text. For related comments see Wachtel 1980.

indirectly signals a commitment to an importantly more fine-grained and demanding assessment of an object's length, and thereby renders contextually relevant a set of standards and criteria that play no role in the everyday setting for my utterance of (11).[8]

Although undoubtedly in need of refinement, the picture sketched in the foregoing paragraph points towards the solution of the semantic puzzle raised by the case of the utterances of (11) and (12) introduced above. Recall that, in the setting for the former utterance, what is required for the truth of a sentence of the form 'a is n cm long' is that a's dimension be included within n and $(n - 0.5\text{ cm})$. More formally, this amounts to the claim that, given the index appropriate to contexts of this type, and given that the table's length is indeed between 120 and 119.5 cm, the point of evaluation which the index determines is one at which that object is truly describable by means of the predicate 'is 120 cm long'. In other words, with respect to the decision put forth by the point i_W, the *demonstratum* of i belongs to the extension of the predicate 'is 120 cm long'. The situation is importantly different with scenarios involving more demanding standards of measurement: given the indexes mirroring contexts of this type, and given that the table's length is not included within the interval between 120 and 119.999 cm, the description 'is 120 cm long' is *not* applicable to that object. By the same token, given such indexes, and given that the table is 119.998 cm long, the predicate involved in your utterance of (12)—namely, 'is more than 119.999 cm long'—misdescribes the *demonstratum*. That your utterance turns out to be false, and mine to be true, is thus hardly incompatible with the reasonable contention that the sentence I employed, (11), logically entails (12): for the

---

[8] The phenomenon in question, roughly falling under the label of *accommodation*, has been discussed in detail in Lewis 1979, independently of the peculiarities of judgements of measurement.

The Vagaries of Action ~ 115

resulting conclusions of truth-value are obtained only by appealing to significantly distinct indexes.

The situation in this respect is thus importantly similar to that with (8) and (9). In this case as well, issues pertaining to the interpretation of indexical expressions, such as 'this table' or the verb's present tense, do not occupy centre stage: the indexes appropriate to the semantic representation of our utterances include the same *demonstratum*, the table at the furniture store, and roughly the same time. Still, it is the involvement of distinct indexes that explains how utterances of (11) may be true, but utterances of a sentence entailed by (11) may be false: the very act of uttering (12) is responsible for the fact that a distinct point of evaluation is determined as contextually relevant, in a manner not wholly dissimilar from that invoked in the analysis of (8), a few paragraphs ago. What *is* different, of course, is that utterances of (8) are more overtly and unquestionably responsible for significant effects upon the way things happen to be: the very act of uttering (8) may affect the history of the speaker's employment of honorifics, but the sheer utterance of (12) does not determine an objective change in the table's dimensions. But this undeniable difference should not obscure the fact that, although the table did not undergo changes in its size, the contextual shift generated by your use of (12) does determine the way in which the table's length is being assessed: in one case, what matters is the relationship between the piece of furniture in question and a coarsely gauged rod, in the other case what is of relevance is its relationship to a distinct standard of measurement.[9]

---

[9] Salience may be employed not only as relevant to the establishment of *demonstrata*. For instance, utterances of 'Everyone is a liberal' may be uttered truly as a comment at a Socialist convention, but may not truly be followed by an utterance of, say, 'George Bush is a liberal'. This obviously hardly impinges on the validity of the rule of universal exemplification (see Gauker 1997b).

7. Where Am I Now?

This book's main topic is the traditional treatment of meaning and truth, and its relationships to particular instances involving the use of language. As I explained, my label 'traditional' alludes to the essential features of the interpretive systems commonly developed within the tradition of so-called natural language semantics. Still, this label is not meant in a statistical or commemorative sense: as has emerged in the first three chapters of this book, I end up disagreeing with important figures within the standard paradigm on a variety of important issues. Such disagreement is indeed further proof of the urgency of the questions I take up: if even the founding fathers of the traditional approach to indexical languages go astray in their treatment of meaning and truth, it is hardly surprising that less sympathetic philosophers ground their anti-traditionalist stance on important misunderstandings of the standard paradigm's commitments and structure. It is to the misunderstandings promoted by a contemporary form of anti-traditionalism that I turn in the next chapter.

Thus far, I have focused mainly on questions having to do with the items taken into consideration by the interpretive system: namely, clause–index pairs, and with their connections with given utterances. In particular, in Chapter 2, I discussed the interface between contexts and indexes—that is, between the settings in which an utterance takes place and the collections of co-ordinates appropriate for the evaluation of indexical expressions. In this chapter, I addressed some questions related to the traditional notion that semantic interpretation be carried out with respect to pairs including an index and an expression-type, rather than along the lines suggested by the token-reflexive approach. A recurrent theme in both chapters has to do with the system's choices regarding matters of logic, and with their distinction from issues pertaining to the truth-values of certain utterances.

In the next chapter, I turn to a complementary question, pertaining to the *outputs* yielded by traditional systems: namely, t-distributions, and to their relationship with certain important features of utterances, in particular their truth-conditions. The discussion of this issue centres around a fashionable version of anti-traditionalist scepticism, the contextualist current I already discussed briefly in the final sections of Chapter 1. There, I questioned the contextualists' considerations regarding disambiguation and reference assignment, and some of their comments on 'pure' indexicals and demonstratives. Still, as I explicitly recognized, these themes represent only a preliminary stab within the contextualist strategy, relatively independent of their central argument. It is the unsoundness of this argument that I aim to unveil in Chapter 4.

Chapter 4
The Colour of the Leaves

CONSIDER the story of Pia, adapted from Travis (1997). Pia's Japanese maple has russet leaves; she paints them green. Addressing her neighbour, a photographer looking for a green subject, she says, apparently truly:

(1) The leaves are green.

Imagine now that Pia's botanist friend is interested in green leaves for her dissertation and that, in reply, Pia utters (1) again. This time, her utterance seems intuitively false.

Why be interested in Pia's story? Because, at least according to some, its analysis 'would seem to have considerable and exciting consequences for semantics' (Travis 1985: 188). The reason for excitement consists in the vindication of contextualism, a sceptical attitude towards the treatment of meaning and truth sketched in Chapter 1. For, so the story goes, it follows from Pia's case that 'all that meaning fixes allows for words to state truth, but also falsehood, of given items in given conditions' (Travis 1996: 453), a conclusion allegedly incompatible with a core assumption of traditional approaches: namely, 'the axiom that the literal meaning of a sentence determines a set of truth conditions' (Searle 1980: 227).

The contextualist literature abounds with cases presumably parallel to Travis's story of Pia. This wealth of examples is not accidental. The contextualist strategy is grounded in the presentation of counter-examples to the aforementioned 'axiom'—that is, on the identification of utterances with respect to which our intuitions of meaning and truth supposedly do not conform to the results yielded by traditional interpretive systems. But intuitions are not always indisputable. Indeed, with respect to *some* of the examples in the literature, my own reactions are rather lukewarm. Take another of Travis's stories, that of the man who weighs 79 kilos naked in the morning, and 82 kilos after a large meal (Travis 1985). Obviously, utterances of 'The man weighs 79 kilos' will turn out to be true in one case but false in another. Still, this is hardly more surprising than the notion that, say, 'Felix is on the mat' is true when uttered as a description of a feline on a rug, but false if the animal hopped on to the table: after the man has put on weight, what was once true turns out not to be true any more.

But the contextualist attack is not so easily disposed of. Even though not all examples may be equally convincing, a wide variety of other cases seems to make the point in a rather persuasive manner. Even though, in Austin's words, 'it cannot be expected that all examples will appeal equally to all hearers' (Austin 1961: 12), at least *some* of the contextualist instances ought to be taken seriously. Pia's case strikes me as a fairly prima-facie convincing attempt in this direction, and I shall adopt it as my principal target in this chapter. The reader who disagrees with my penchant for painted leaves is invited to adapt my considerations to instances he or she finds more convincing. Inevitably, before I conclude this chapter, I will also address that most widely discussed example: utterances of 'It is raining' taking place at different locations.

1. The Road from the Forties

Here is a slightly caricatural but not entirely inaccurate reproduction of the historical picture occasionally painted by contemporary contextualists. Once upon a time, so the story goes, a few nerdy philosophers began to lay the foundation for what would later be known as 'natural language semantics'. Their stereotypically nerdy image derived from the deleterious combination of two intellectual traits: they were pretty good at mathematics and, at least judging from the content of their writings, obscenely inept at social linguistic exchange. Unsurprisingly, so we are told, the picture of language that emerged from their approach worked pretty well for complex non-colloquial examples such as

> if zero has a certain property, and if whenever a number has a property its successor has it too, then all numbers have that property,

but performed very poorly when it came to even the simplest examples in the vernacular—say, 'I love you', 'The leaves are green', or 'Show me the money'. At best, whenever everyday speech had to be taken into account, the nerdy philosophers' attention confined itself pathetically to a very restricted and contrived class of exemplars—chief among all, the by now infamous case of 'The cat is on the mat'. It took no longer than a couple of decades before someone with a good deal of common sense pointed out that love letters and monetary demands were more central to the process of language exchange than the statement of mathematical induction or the description of a feline's predilection for carpets. Still, with the exception of a few occasional concessions regarding this or that detail, nerdy semanticists remained singularly indifferent to the fundamental questions raised by their more urbane challengers. As a result, so the story ends, the emerging paradigm within natural language semantics remains founded on importantly mistaken assumptions, worthy to be brought to the attention of hopefully more receptive younger generations.

A picture along the foregoing line often emerges from the writings of contextualists with pedigree ambitions. François Recanati, for instance, writes:

> Around the middle of the twentieth century, there were two opposing camps within the analytic philosophy of language. The first camp—ideal language philosophy, as it was then called—was that of the pioneers, Frege, Russell, Carnap, Tarski, etc. They were, first and foremost, logicians studying formal languages and, through them, 'language' in general. They were not originally concerned with natural language, which they thought defective in various ways; yet, in the sixties, some of their disciples established the relevance of their methods to the detailed study of natural language (Montague [1968], Davidson 1984)... The other camp was that of so-called ordinary language philosophers, who thought important features of natural language were not revealed but hidden by the logical approach initiated by Frege and Russell. (Recanati 2002b: 1)

Chief among the aspects allegedly 'hidden by the logical approach' is the role which context plays within the interface between meaning and truth. Contrary to the evidence available to anyone sufficiently sensitive to the subtleties of natural languages, so we are told, the logicians rested satisfied with too simple-minded a picture: 'Central in the ideal language tradition had been the equation of, or at least the close connection between, the meaning of a sentence and its truth conditions' (Recanati 2002b: 1). The reason why the traditionalists' connection between meaning and truth is taken to be too close has to do with their inability to leave room for contextual contributions. So, for Robyn Carston, it is a characteristic of the ideal language tradition associated with Frege and Russell that the 'extrapolation from the properties of fully explicit, content-invariant logical languages to the properties of natural languages had led to a gross underestimation of the context-sensitivity of natural language utterances' (Carston 2002: 3).[1]

A not dissimilar diagnosis had already been made by Travis in a series of papers that pioneered the new wave of the contextualist movement. For Travis, not unlike Carston and Recanati, hints in an anti-traditionalist vein were already clearly audible in the Forties, especially in the work of Wittgenstein and Austin, and were directed precisely against the view of meaning and truth-conditions which I sketched in Chapter 1. The positive side of the coin, once again, had to do with the insistence on the peculiarities of each occasion of speaking, i.e., on the importance of what are commonly known as contextual factors.

The story begins in a period encapsulating the second world war... Around then, it began to be argued with force that an expression... while it well might *mean* something, does not *say* anything... What would be said in one such speaking is not quite the same as what would be said in another. (Travis 1985: 187–8)

For the record, I find the snippets of philosophical history embedded in the passages I just quoted highly debatable. Just to cite one example among many, it seems at least questionable to insist that Frege, of all people, 'was not originally concerned with natural language', because he thought it 'defective' in ways that put it beyond the philosopher's area of inquiry. By the same token, it must surely be incorrect to insist that, when looking at natural languages, Frege was 'extrapolating from context-invariant languages'. Ironically, precisely one of the passages occasionally presented as testimony to Frege's presumed disdain for the vernacular indicates that he was well aware of at least one important source of contextual dependence—so much so,

---

[1] In a personal communication, Carston confirms my suspicion that 'content-invariant' is either a typo for, or a locution synonymous with, 'context-invariant': a 'content-invariant' language is one in which semantic content may be determined without relativization to contextual parameters.

The Colour of the Leaves ~ 123

indeed, that he ended up providing one of the most widely discussed theories of indexicality.

> The sentences of our everyday language leave a good deal to guesswork. It is the surrounding circumstances that enable us to make the right guess. The sentence I utter does not always contain everything that is necessary; a great deal has to be supplied by the context, by the gestures I make and the direction of my eyes. But a language that is intended for scientific employment must not leave anything to guesswork. (Frege 1914: 213)

What a passage of this kind is symptomatic of is a perhaps questionable view of what is required for 'scientific employment'. What it surely does not reveal is its author's presumed desire to abandon, regiment, or misrepresent natural language's contextual sensitivity.

Still, it is not on the boring questions of scholarly exegesis that I intend to focus in what follows, but on the more exciting assessment of the polemical intent that motivates the quotes from Recanati, Carston, and Travis. Let us, then, put aside the question of whether the modern strands of contextualism do indeed pursue the directions first envisioned in the late Forties, and whether they do echo presumably well-rehearsed challenges to the Frege-inspired tradition. What remains the case is that, in the last two decades or so, a variety of otherwise quite distinct philosophical projects have come to a concordant sceptical conclusion, directed towards the view of meaning and truth introduced in Chapter 1. According to the contextualists, and regardless of the very important distinction between alternative views within the traditional paradigm (say, the very obvious difference between the Montagovian tradition and the Davidsonian programme), something rotten lies at the very foundation of the traditional semantic edifice.

It should be pointed out at the outset that, at least in many cases, the content of the contextualists' considerations is by no means limited to their attack on mainstream semantics. Their work contains a variety of considerations pertaining, among other things, to the theory of communication, the Gricean take on pragmatics, and the cognitive structures involved in language understanding. Unsurprisingly, then, the few authors I collected under the label of 'contextualism' disagree with each other on a variety of topics they deem to be of primary importance, and may well not recognize themselves as members of a unique and well-organized school of thought. Still, Recanati, Carston, and Travis (together with Dan Sperber, Deirdre Wilson, Ann Bezuidenhout, Diane Blakemore, and others) pursue a relatively consistent, common strategy against the paradigm I introduced in Chapter 1, in particular for reasons having to do with the theory of meaning and truth presupposed within standard interpretive systems.[2] To a lesser extent, as I already explained, their attack focuses (unsuccessfully, if my considerations in Chapter 1 are correct) on 'preparatory' questions such as ellipsis unpacking, ambiguity resolution, and reference assignment. But a much more central and well-developed direction in their strategy pertains more directly to questions of meaning and truth, and to the applicability of traditional systems to actual instances of language use. It is this aspect of the contextualist challenge that I discuss in this chapter.

2. The Contextualist Challenge

So, let us agree that we intuitively accept as true Pia's utterance *u* to the photographer, but not her utterance *v* to the botanist. What is supposed to follow from this initial inclination, at least once certain further assumptions have been taken for granted?

---

[2] See Bezuidenhout 1996 and 1997; Blakemore 2002; Carston 1988 and forthcoming; Recanati 2001; Sperber and Wilson 1995; Wilson and Sperber 1981.

Here is a plausible claim that I am more than willing to grant the contextualists: in the absence of independent arguments to the contrary, on any empirically adequate account, *u* should come out true, and *v* should come out false. That is to say, *u* and *v* do differ in truth-conditions: one is true, the other is false, given one unique way the plant happens to be. Here is another claim that seems to have some initial plausibility, and that I shall not dispute in what follows: both *u* and *v* are utterances of one and the same (non-ambiguous, non-elliptical) sentence, performed by one speaker at times and locations which, for all purposes, may well be envisioned as identical. That is to say: when it comes to the representations appropriate for *u* and *v*, a clause such as

[[the leaves]$_{NP}$[are green]$_{VP}$]$_S$

paired with one and the same set of parameters for the interpretation of any relevant indexical expression is appropriate in either case. But, so the contextualists point out, when conjoined with the procedures embedded in traditional interpretive systems, these plausible claims yield a contradiction. If both *u* and *v* are represented uniformly, it follows from traditional systems that they end up with the same truth-value at any given point, in apparent contrast with the demand that, given one fixed way things happen to be, *u* and *v* differ in truth-value. Barring *ad hoc* denials of the aforementioned additional hypotheses, so it is concluded, it is the system's approach that must be relinquished.

The problem, according to the contextualist diagnosis, is that the traditional standpoint remains obstinately indifferent to a multitude of semantically relevant contributions of context. Even bracketing the simple forms of contextual dependence which customary interpretive systems are willing to acknowledge, so the story goes, the evaluation of one utterance in one setting rather than another makes an unequivocally semantic difference, in that it affects the utterance's truth-conditional profile. As Travis puts is, given an expression

with its meaning (unambiguously) fixed, there are a variety of distinct...things to be said in using it on some production of it or other. What would be said in one such speaking is not quite the same as what would be said in another, at least in the sense that in different speakings, different things would be said to be so (of something), distinguishable in the sense that any one such thing might well be so while the others are not. (Travis 1985: 187–8)

An assessment along these lines has generated a great deal of excitement, matched by a wealth of labels calling attention to the presumably central phenomenon it highlights. What traditionalists stubbornly refuse to acknowledge, so we are told, is a process of contextually determined content *enrichment*: the message encoded in an utterance, and *a fortiori* its truth-conditions, are richer than the outcome presented by traditional systems. On this view, then, going down the good old strictly compositional route leaves you either with truth-conditionally incomplete results or, at best, with conclusions that are indeed interpretable in truth-conditional terms, but correspond to intuitively wrong truth-conditions. The missing items which context is supposed to supply, so as to satisfy the need for appropriate truth-conditional outcomes, are sometimes called *unarticulated constituents*—constituents of semantic content that nobody bothered to articulate. The resulting picture is then accorded the catchy appellation *truth-conditional pragmatics*: contextual phenomena that presumably fall within the province of pragmatics do make a difference to truth-conditions, against the presumed traditional picture of the process of interpretation, sealed off from anything less rigorous than clause–index pairs. What all this allegedly unveils is thus the essential *underdeterminacy* of meaning: fix an expression's meaning (and whatever meaning explicitly requires—say, the co-ordinates in the index), and you still have not done enough to provide truth-conditional conclusions, or, at least, the *right* truth-conditional conclusions.[3]

Labels are not explanations, but often serve the useful purpose of calling attention to presumably not so obvious phenomena. Part of my problem with the contextualist challenge is that the phenomena in question seem indeed obvious. Everybody (with the exception perhaps of a few misguided traditionalists, on whom more later) knows that you can make true colour remarks to a photographer but not to a botanist, even on the assumption that neither your subject nor the meaning of your expressions has changed. And everybody must surely be familiar with the fact that, even if you weigh 79 kg early in the morning, you may on some occasions truly utter 'I weigh 82 kg'. Indeed, more than a few traditionalists, at least until recently, seem not to have taken these commonplace observations as calamitous for their take on language: as Travis complained a couple of decades ago, 'as for semantics, the majority reaction [to the contextualist challenge] ...among philosophers at least has always been as if it never happened' (Travis 1985: 191). As indicated both by the wealth of variations within the contextualist standpoint and by the frantic responses of some contemporary sympathizers with the traditional approach, the spirit of the times must finally have come to terms with painted leaves and similar stories.

The main target of this chapter is not the content of the contextualist viewpoint, but its polemical intent. I have no qualms whatsoever with the contextualist claim that, for instance, Pia's utterances differ in truth-conditions, and that, in this sense, conventional meaning does not 'determine a set of truth-conditions'. But I have not the slightest sympathy for interpretations of such a rather unexciting conclusion in the apocalyptic spirit promoted within the contextualist camp. In particular, contrary to an assumption that some contemporary

---

[3] See e.g. Carston 2002; Recanati 2002*c* and 2003. See also Bianchi 2001*b*.

traditionalists are all too willing to concede to their adversaries, the sense in which meaning fails to 'determine a set of truth conditions' is by no means at odds with an 'axiom' of the mainstream approach to natural languages. Traditional systems of the type presented in Chapter 1, so I argue, are perfectly equipped for dealing with Pia's scenarios in an intuitively satisfactory manner.

3. Tradition Strikes Back

As I mentioned above, the contextualist case against mainstream systems is grounded on certain intuitions, conjoined with a few plausible additional assumptions. Recall, for instance, the case of *u* and *v*, the utterances of 'The leaves are green' directed respectively to the photographer and to the botanist. Concisely, here is the argumentative line motivating the contextualists' enthusiasm.

(i) Interpretive systems of the type presented in Chapter 1, coupled with appropriate hypotheses pertaining to the representation of *u* and *v*, assign the same t-distribution to *u* and *v*.

(ii) If two utterances *u* and *v* have intuitively distinct truth-conditions, then any empirically adequate interpretive system ought to assign distinct t-distributions to *u* and *v*.

(iii) *u* and *v* have intuitively distinct truth-conditions.

(c) Hence, interpretive systems of the type presented in Chapter 1 are empirically inadequate.

Mesmerized by the contextualist strategy, and unwilling to relinquish the presumably unquestionable transition in (ii), some contemporary defenders of the traditional paradigm have unhesitatingly embraced a standard philosophical defensive strategy: if your attack on my favourite thesis assumes some (no matter how plausible) additional premisses, so the strategy goes, what you end up presenting is nothing but a counter-argument against one or another of them—in our case, a *reductio* of (i) or (iii). Not an *independent* counter-argument, mind you: in our case, not, say, the thesis that syntactic motivations provide autonomous reasons for representing u and v in terms of distinct clause–index pairs, or the claim that pollution-induced neurophysiologic deficiencies make us unreliable judges of truth and falsity. What emerges, rather, is the immovable conviction that, since both (ii) and the traditional approach must be correct, either (i) or (iii) must be on the wrong track.

Let me begin with the attack on (iii): namely, with the suggestion that traditional systems may be salvaged by challenging the reliability of certain initial pre-theoretical conclusions of truth-conditions. Still, examples such as Pia's are not, or at least not obviously, cases in which our intuitions of truth-value are systematically mistaken—for instance, because we fail to identify the literal point of the utterance and focus instead on some information the speaker is merely hinting at. Of course, that this is not *obviously* the case does not immediately entail that an explanation along these lines is untenable. There are, after all, relatively surprising cases in which systematic mistakes of this type may indeed take place—the oft-cited instance being our assessment of the truth-value of 'Tonto jumped on his horse and rode away' in cases in which he first rode away (say, on his motorcycle) and then jumped on the horse. As Mark Richard notes, '[e]xamples like that concerning "and" and temporal order help make the point that what seems for all the world like a truth-conditional implication may turn out not to be one' (Richard 1990b: 123; cited in Carston 2002: 223). For the record, the 'oft-cited instance' strikes me as grounded on not fully convincing arguments pertaining to the semantic profile of the expressions in the Tonto sentence. But my views on 'and' (and on the verbs' tenses) are of no immediate relevance here. What is important, rather, is that *arguments* uncontroversially need to be put forward in favour of the somewhat unexpected conclusion that no claim of temporal succession is literally put forth by utterances of some 'and' sentences. One needs to *argue* that, for instance, the price of including temporal relations as part of the meaning of 'and' is too steep, and that independent mechanisms—say, the effects of some conversational maxim or another—are such that competent speakers' unreflective responses often get the truth-value wrong. As I explain in what follows, I am less than convinced by how some traditionalists have tried to defend a strategy of this type with respect to the case of Pia.

Jonathan Berg supports the aforementioned anti-contextualist line by focusing on another among Travis's examples, one involving utterances of 'There's milk in the refrigerator' *vis-à-vis* an empty fridge with a small puddle of milk on one of its shelves (Travis 1989). During a discussion about the availability of beverages, so Travis points out, an utterance of this sentence seems false; when occurring as part of a dispute on how well the fridge has been cleaned, on the other hand, it appears to be true. Berg disagrees:

the sentence is true in *both* of the given contexts. Although [it] might *seem* false in the context where the hearer is interested in getting milk for his coffee, that is only because uttering the sentence in that context is likely to be misleading. (Berg 2002: 353)

Why is it likely to be misleading, and, in particular, why is its literal message to be evaluated in terms of truth? A footnote reminds the reader of 'Grice's classic examples of conversational implicature'—i.e., of examples involving the distinction between semantically encoded content and merely conversationally imparted information. In the same vein, when considering the objection that her views of truth-conditions contrast with certain rather firm intuitions, Emma Borg replies:

The Colour of the Leaves ~ 131

as we all know thanks to Grice, because a speaker means a proposition *p* by her utterance of a sentence *s*, this does not necessarily mean that the sentence uttered should be treated as having the semantic value that p. (Borg forthcoming: 156–7)[4]

But how exactly (or even not so exactly) is this supposed to work? Is it a classic case of 'hinting' that, say, there is a sufficient quantity of milk, while officially saying only that the fridge contains a non-null amount of milk molecules? And how is this strategy supposed to work in Pia's case? Are both *u* and *v* true, with the latter misleadingly indicating that greenness is of a botanically appropriate type, or are they both false, with the former hinting that the greenness-fascinated photographer is likely to be satisfied with the officially non-green leaves? At least with respect to this latter question, Marc Sainsbury suggests a reply on the traditionalist's behalf:

I suggest that 'Those leaves are green' is true in both cases, but that in the first a participant who came to learn that it is true would jump to the conclusion that it is made true in the normal way, rather than the exceptional way. This participant would be led astray; but one can easily be led astray by the truth. (Sainsbury 2001: 403)

Why truth? Why not insist that, say, a plant's true colour is the one nature dictated, so that attributions of greenness to a russet Japanese maple are inevitably false? One can be led astray by the truth, but one can just as easily be put on the right track by the untrue. And, more generally, what are the reasons for embracing either route, i.e., for claiming that exactly one truth-value must be the right one?

The answer to these questions emerges with admirable frankness in Berg's essay a few paragraphs after the somewhat unenthusiastic appeal to conversational implicatures, when it is admitted that at least some of the contextualist examples are

---

[4] For considerations in the direction of the distinction between semantic content and speaker's meaning, see also Borg 2004 and Saul 2002*a* and 2002*b*.

indeed 'hard cases' for the standard approach to semantics. But 'hard cases might just be hard cases, not counterexamples... And despite the many hard cases facing [the standard view of semantics] there is no alternative... facing fewer hard cases' (Berg 2002: 354). At this stage, the point is no longer that an independently motivated apparatus—say, Grice's analysis of hinting—yields the desired result. The point is, rather, that, from a methodological point of view, we had better be ready to swallow admittedly 'startling' conclusions, in particular that

> competent speakers do not always know what they are saying.... Startling as this claim might seem, its proof lies in the well-known fact that competent speakers sometimes disagree about semantic content. Russell and Strawson, for instance, were eminently competent speakers of English, yet they disagreed about the semantic content of sentences such as 'The Present King of France is bald'. (Berg 2002: 354)

For the record, Russell and Strawson did not disagree about semantic content in the manner of relevance here. If Russell and Strawson approached 'The present king of France is bald' with contrasting pre-theoretic inclinations, their dispute would be of no greater interest than the historical record of the great men's diverging intuitions. The difference in their treatment of 'the' is the result of *arguments* (pertaining to the status of certain logical laws, to general principles about reference, and so on), rather than a brute fact of intuitions. So, what exactly is the argument supporting the notion that, for instance, v is after all true but conversationally misleading? Is it just that, in the absence of alternatives, we'd better stick to traditional systems and learn to live with 'hard cases'?

Premiss (iii) is not the only hypothesis that contextualists employ (together with the hereto undisputed claim in (ii)) in order to transform their intuitions into a counter-argument against traditional interpretive systems. Consequently, traditionalists unwilling to disregard the truth-conditional significance of

Pia's tale have directed their aim towards another crucial premiss in the contextualist argument, namely (i). Their reasoning is admirable in its unwavering confidence in the traditional paradigm: since u and v do indeed differ in truth-conditions, and since this difference must be reflected by the assignment of alternative t-distributions, careful analysis of Pia's utterances must inevitably unveil one or another among the well-known mechanisms which, in the hands of the interpretive system, motivate an assignment of this type. On this view, then, what must emerge, one way or another, is an account in which the expressions involved in the analysis of u and v either differ in meaning or display the type of meaning characteristic of indexicality.

In views of the former type, distinct clauses must figure in the appropriate representations of Pia's utterances. Hypotheses in this spirit include the assumption that u, unlike v, includes something along the lines of, say, 'The surface of the leaves is green', or the suggestion that u, unlike v, involves the disambiguation of the allegedly ambiguous 'is green' as [are green$_1$]$_{VP}$, interpreted as addressing the colour of an object's outermost surface (or something in this vein). Though different in many important details, both suggestions agree that the difference in the truth-conditional profile of Pia's utterances is to be accounted for in terms of a discrepancy in meaning: if the expressions within the clauses appropriate for the representation of u and v are conventionally assigned distinct meanings, the divergence in these utterances' truth-conditions is obviously accountable within a customary approach in terms of t-distributional discrepancy. Treatments unwilling to swallow hypotheses of ambiguity, ellipsis, and the like embrace the indexicality route: the needed difference in t-distributions, conjoined with a hypothesis of uniform meaning, is now interpreted as entailing the assignment of non-constant characters to at least some of the expressions under study. Thus, on this view, what Pia's scenario shows is that some expression in (the clause corresponding to) (1), presumably [be green]$_{VP}$, is an indexical: for instance, the semantic value of [be green]$_{VP}$ with respect to an index i and a point k is taken to be the set of objects x such that x is green in k with respect to the 'purpose of colour' parameter in i (or something along these lines). When equipped with such hypotheses of indexicality, so this proposal concludes, the traditional apparatus may deal with cases such as Pia's without relinquishing the customary understanding of meaning and truth.[5]

At least in their initial form, these responses seem hopelessly *ad hoc*. No independent motivation seems to support the theses that the sentences employed by Pia are the result of a process of ellipsis or that any of the words they contain is ambiguous in the desired manner. Similarly, no item in (1) seems to be an indexical of the right kind—that is, one responsible for truth-value shifts such as those encountered in Pia's scenario. As Travis points out,

> It is part of the meaning of 'I', and its use in English, that it is a device for a speaker to speak of himself.... By contrast, it is not part of what 'green' means, so far as we can tell, that speakings of it speak of, or refer to, such-and-such parameters.... The parameter approach does not *automatically* suggest itself here as it did with 'I'. (Travis 1997: 93)

These tentative remarks may of course be overturned by the discovery of *independent* evidence favouring an indexical analysis

---

[5] A parallel hypothesis, though in many respects different from the assumption of indexicality, is Zoltan Gendler Szabó's notion that expressions such as 'is green' be associated with a variable, whose semantic evaluation is sensitive to the relevant features of context (for Szabó's well-taken remarks against the indexical view, see Szabó 2001: 125). But Szabó underestimates the import of Travis's puzzle, referring to it as a 'limited phenomenon' restricted to adjectives such as 'green', 'smart', or 'good' (Szabó 2001: 122–6): see later in the text and n. 8 for a more realistic assessment of the pervasiveness of the phenomenon. The extension of Szabó's proposal needed to take care of all relevant examples would thus yield an unlikely manifold of hidden variables, accompanying all sorts of expressions. As Szabó eventually concedes, his strategy 'is likely to lead to a lexicon where many, perhaps most entries contain contextual variables' (Szabó 2001: 138). See also Bach 2000; Neale 2000; Partee 1989; Stanley 2000, 2002*a*, and 2002*b*; Stanley and Szabo 2000*a* and 2000*b*.

of colour predicates (in the sense relevant for our scenarios), or a treatment of (1) in terms of ellipsis or ambiguity.[6] But the burden is squarely on the traditionalists' side: none of the hypotheses entertained thus far is, as it stands, a comfortable stance to take.

More importantly for the assessment of the rejection of (i), the challenge put forth by Pia's case may easily be reproduced in a variety of cases that do not involve expressions of colour or the assessment of an object tint. On an invitation to the ambassador's party it says 'Formal attire required'. I show up in a sporty suit with a tie, and they lend me a tuxedo. Later that evening, back in my suit, I show up at a restaurant where it says 'Formal attire required', and they let me in. The sentence 'My attire is formal', used by me as a description of one and the same suit, may thus apparently be uttered truly at the restaurant, but not at the party. During a discussion of human intelligence, you point out that only our species routinely employs vehicles for the conveyance of goods or people. I indicate a baby carriage and remark, truly, 'That is a vehicle'. Pushing that very same stroller, we encounter a sign saying 'No vehicles allowed after this point'; I say, truly, 'This is not a vehicle', and keep walking. The sentence 'That is a vehicle', directed towards one and the same item, is thus utterable as a true description of it on one occasion, but not on another. When discussing with my neighbour the boundary between our properties, I point at the contraption of twine and sticks surrounding my garden and say, 'Everything on this side of the fence is mine'. Later that day, when commenting on the sorry state of my backyard, I concede: 'I should build a fence'. An utterance of 'That is a fence', said while pointing at one and the

---

[6] By 'indexical analysis' I mean of course an analysis yielding results relevant for the case under discussion. For instance, there may well be arguments favouring an approach to 'is green' according to which that predicate stands for different properties when employed to describe pens ('produces green inscriptions') rather than coats ('is green on most of its surface'); see e.g. Lahav 1989. Considerations of this kind are idle with respect to Pia's story, however, where what is at issue is the greenness of leaves.

same object, seems true in the former scenario, but false in the other. *Modulo* some not too important differences, these examples support the conclusion reached by the contextualist assessment of Pia's uses of (1): utterances of one and the same sentence are apparently endowed with distinct truth-conditions even on the assumption of a fixed interpretation of the overt indexicals they involve. So, if the analyses of Pia's scenario sketched above were on the right track, their application to the cases in this paragraph would result in an improbable multiplication of ambiguity, covert indexicality, or ellipsis.[7]

The central aim of this chapter is to neutralize the contextualist challenge against the traditional paradigm. For this reason, I could afford to be relatively dismissive of certain anti-contextualist positions that I am not willing to embrace. As a result, nothing in what I said thus far is intended as a conclusive counter-argument in favour of premisses (i) or (iii) in the contextualist reasoning presented above. Those disappointed (or, depending on one's tendencies, emboldened) by the absence of knock-down refutations of appeals to conversational implicatures or hidden indexicality are invited, however, to consider with an open mind the positive side of my anti-contextualist strategy, presented in the remainder of this chapter. There I argue that the widespread conviction that anti-contextualism entails the rejection of either (i) or (iii) puts an unnecessary burden on the

---

[7] According to Szabó, 'there is a trivial way that the example [of Pia] can be generalized... Take the sentence "The book is a novel." There are all sorts of borderline instances of novelhood... This is not especially interesting' (Szabó 2001: 125). The examples I proposed involve predicates such as 'is formal' or 'is a vehicle' no less vague than 'is a novel'. Yet, the fact that these expressions' extensions (and, for that matter, the extension of 'is green') have fuzzy boundaries is not relevant here: just as Pia's leaves are unquestionably categorized as green on one occasion but not on the other, a stroller clearly falls among vehicles in one scenario, but not in the other. What is interesting from the present purpose is not the mere possibility of borderline cases, but rather the contextually sensitive shifts in the location of the boundary (see also Lewis 1979).

The Colour of the Leaves ~ 137

traditionalist's shoulders. The burden is unnecessary because, as I explain in the next sections, the contextualist argument may be blocked naturally by challenging another of its premisses, namely (ii). Still, the reasons for scepticism with respect to (ii) may emerge only after certain broader questions have been addressed, pertaining to the traditional understanding of meaning and truth. It is for this reason that I temporarily abandon the case of Pia and her painted leaves, and focus on general issues pertaining to the interpretive system's treatment of truth and meaning, and to the application of its results to particular instances of language use.

4. Method: Intuitions, Utterances, and the System

A crucial criterion for the assessment of an interpretive system's interest and tenability is its *empirical adequacy*: what is desired is that it yield results compatible with the intuitions of competent, intelligent speakers, or at least with those intuitions that we are willing to recognize as relevant. But such intuitions do not directly pertain to the mapping of abstract pairs with t-distributions: rather, they concern the conditions under which utterances of certain expressions on particular occasions turn out to be true. For instance, we are inclined to judge an utterance of 'Felix is on the mat' as true whenever Felix is indeed on the mat, but not if, say, he is sitting on the table. Competent speakers' intuitions thus yield evaluations of particular utterances, while entertaining certain hypotheses about the way things may be: we may be invited to consider an utterance of 'Felix is on the mat' while imagining that Felix is on the table—that is, we may be invited to indulge in the thought-experiment involving that utterance and that (actual or merely imaginary) situation. Remaining deliberately neutral with respect to metaphysical questions regarding the ontological status and structure of such 'ways things may be',

I shall hereafter refer to the conditions of certain items, such as Felix's whereabouts, as a *worldly condition*. In this manner, competent speakers may be tested for their intuitions about the *truth-conditions* of an utterance: that is, about its truth-value with respect to alternative worldly conditions.

So, the intuitions of interest from this essay's point of view have to do with the truth-conditional profile of utterances, rather than with the more austere t-distributions that interpretive systems associate with their inputs. In Chapter 2 I paused on the relationships between the objects of our intuitive assessment, utterances, and the system's inputs, clause–index pairs. There I explained how, once a particular hypothesis of representation is taken for granted, the system's results may be interpreted as an assignment of t-distributions to utterances. At least taking for granted that hypotheses of ellipsis, lexical ambiguity, or indexicality are not of immediate relevance with respect to the case of Pia, no further attention needs to be devoted to the choice of the clauses and of the parameters in the indexes appropriate for either u or v, her utterances of 'The leaves are green' directed to the photographer and the botanist. In what follows I thus speak simply of the t-distribution which the system directly assigns to these utterances, even though, rigorously speaking, such an assignment is relativized to a particular hypothesis of representation.

Still, the interface between systems and intuitions remains worthy of closer scrutiny: even granting appropriate assumptions about the representation r of an utterance u, what is required of an empirically adequate interpretive system is that, when applied to r, it yields an outcome compatible with our intuitions regarding u. But the comparison between the system's verdict and such intuitions is not trivial. As I explained, what the interpretive system yields are results in terms of t-distributions—that is, truth-values across points of evaluation, and, derivatively, conclusions of unrelativized truth-value on the basis of the choice of a privileged point. What our intuitions involve, on the other hand, are decisions pertaining to the truth-values of an utterance on a certain occasion, *vis-à-vis* a particular worldly condition. The comparison between results of t-distributions and truth-conditional verdicts may seem to be of such a trivial nature that no further analysis of this interface is needed. Yet, as I argue in this section, this *nonchalance*, though harmless for a variety of purposes, may be responsible for the inappropriate understanding of a variety of examples, including the tale of Pia's leaves.

For didactic purposes, it is often quite legitimate to ignore the issues pertaining to the relationships between t-distributions and truth-conditions, or to assume that they are of an inconsequential nature. The intuition that u has a truth-value t, given a particular worldly condition w, is thus typically interpreted as the requirement that u be mapped to a t-distribution yielding t for any point 'corresponding to' w. For instance, since your utterance of 'Felix is on the mat' strikes me as false if the cat is on the table, what I require of the system is that it assigns falsehood at any point 'corresponding to' the condition eliciting my verdict, one in which the cat is not where you thought it was. And since your utterance of 'Felix is on the mat' seems to provide a true description of the cat's position whenever he is indeed sleeping on its rug, what I demand is that the system comes out with a verdict of truth *vis-à-vis* any point 'corresponding to' that state of affairs. At least as far as everyday instances of 'Felix is on the mat' go, such correspondence seems straightforward: points, so it seems, are nothing more than mere formal counterparts of ways the world may be, of particular (actual or merely imagined) worldly conditions.

A parallel attitude supports a methodology standardly employed in the comparison of the t-distributional profile of *two* utterances. Take again the aforementioned utterance of 'Felix is on the mat', and contrast it with an utterance of, say,

> The cat you own is on the mat.

If any doubt ensues regarding the difference in the t-distributions that ought to be assigned to these examples, it may easily be dispelled by taking into consideration a certain (perhaps merely possible) worldly condition, one in which Felix is mewing on the fence, and Moe, the cat you bought, is indeed on the mat. With respect to such a scenario, the former utterance is intuitively false, but the latter appears to be true. Hence, so this strategy points out, any adequate system must evaluate one as true, and the other as false, with respect to some unique point of evaluation k: namely, with respect to any point reflecting the scenario just described. In other words, so this strategy concludes, any adequate system should assign distinct t-distributions to the utterances in question. More generally, given two utterances (of different sentences, or of one and the same sentence on different occasions), one typically derives the requirement that they be mapped to distinct t-distributional profiles by means of the following *snapshot strategy*. Consider a particular snapshot of how things happen to be—say, a particular history of certain cats' whereabouts—and keep it unchanged as you shift from one utterance to the other. If one utterance, but not the other, is intuitively evaluated as providing a true description of the way things are, then the application of the system to the former ought to yield a t-distribution different from that associated with the latter.

Still, the aforementioned casual attitude towards the relationship between t-distributions and truth-conditions, though harmless for a variety of pedagogical purposes, bypasses questions that are of immediate relevance with respect to the issue addressed in this chapter. In particular, so I argue in what follows, the resulting snapshot strategy for the identification of the t-distributional outcome required of an adequate system is not inevitably correct: utterances such as Pia's u and v, though unquestionably differing in their truth-conditional profile, may be mapped to identical t-distributions by an empirically suitable system. Hence,

The Colour of the Leaves ~ 141

so I explain, premiss (ii) in the contextualist reasoning against customary approaches, namely the claim that

(ii) If two utterances *u* and *v* have intuitively distinct truth-conditions, then any empirically adequate interpretive system ought to assign distinct t-distributions to *u* and *v*,

must be rejected.

A terminological caveat, making good on a promise from Chapter 1, pertains to the employment of the familiar locution 'possible world'. At least taking for granted certain non-uncontroversial assumptions, points of evaluation are often labelled (and indeed have thus been labelled in some passages in this book) with the help of the 'w'-word: singular terms are associated with a certain referent with respect to this or that (possible) world; sentence–index pairs turn out true at one world, but not at another; etc. This terminological choice is, in itself, unobjectionable: possible worlds, understood as parameters that provide a *definite* answer to questions such as the *denotatum* of a singular term or the truth-value of a sentence are indeed the kind of object desired by the system's internal workings. But there is a colloquial and more widespread sense of 'possible world', as roughly synonymous with 'ways things may be': in this sense, a not uncommon introduction to possible worlds includes the vague gesticulation supposed to indicate the possible world we live in, the actual course of history. Possible worlds, in this sense, turn out to be equivalent to what I labelled 'worldly conditions'. If unnoticed, this ambiguity may be perilous: if possible worlds in the sense of points of evaluation were identical to possible worlds in the sense of worldly conditions, then t-distributions would be truth-conditions, and (ii) would be trivially true. But they are not: as I explain in what follows, worldly conditions, such as the actual way things turned out to be with respect to Pia's plant or my attire, may well fail to supply the kind of definite decisions which points of evaluation are supposed to provide.

Our pre-theoretic reactions regarding the truth-values of particular utterances given (real or imagined) worldly conditions depend, among other things, upon our intuitive understanding of such conditions. One of the reasons why an utterance of 'Felix is on the mat' appears to be true with respect to the actual course of history is that Felix's position intuitively strikes us as being of the on-the-mat type. So, since a central task of the interpretive system is to yield intuitively correct verdicts of truth-value, and since such verdicts are given relative to particular points of evaluation, what is required of an adequate system is that it renders the appropriate truth-value—in this case, truth—with respect to a point of evaluation 'corresponding to' the condition in question, in this case a point in which cat and mat belong to the extension of 'is on'. By the same token, given that an utterance of 'Felix is on the mat' appears to be false *vis-à-vis* an imaginary situation in which Felix is on the table, it is imperative that an empirically suitable interpretive system renders verdicts of falsehood with respect to points of evaluation reflecting this merely possible condition, presumably points at which Felix and the rug are excluded from the extension of 'is on'. For parallel reasons, then, the evaluation of Pia's utterances, or of the other examples presented above, must be assessed by focusing on the truth-values obtained with respect to points corresponding to our intuitive interpretation of the relevant worldly conditions. So, intuitively, how are things with Pia's leaves (or my suit, the nearby stroller, or the contraption in my garden)?

Pia's photographer friend asks for a green subject, and Pia points at the maple tree. For the purpose at hand, the leaves are as good a green exemplar as any: on this occasion, the leaves *count as* green. Later, Pia's botanist neighbour needs green leaves: this time, the leaves are ineligible. If these intuitive judgements on the leaves' colour are given the significance they deserve for the purpose of the pre-theoretically correct assessment of Pia's utterances, it seems inevitable that the required results, truth in one case and falsity in the other, be obtained by taking into consideration distinct points of evaluation. Even though one and the same actual worldly condition faces Pia, one in which the originally russet leaves are covered with green die, her comment to the photographer aims at providing a description of what is intuitively a green-leaves type of situation, whereas her reply to the botanist does not.

A word of caution. Pia's leaves did not change their colour: discolouration or repaint jobs are simply not part of the story. To put it in a metaphysically loaded way: the relationship between the leaves and the property of greenness remains unchanged as we move from Pia's conversation with the photographer to her encounter with the botanist. But the ultimate relationship between the leaves and their colour is beside the point here. What contextualists are concerned with is not the interface between traditional semantics, on the one hand, and the presumed ultimate relationship between the leaves and their greenness (or lack thereof), on the other. After all, if we were assured that, initial appearances notwithstanding, in both scenarios the leaves are in the right (wrong) kind of relationship to that property—that is, that they *really* are (are not) green—then the intuitive assessments of Pia's utterances would not differ in the way needed for the contextualist argument. If you managed to convince me that, say, painting the leaves does not suffice for altering their true colour, then my conviction that Pia's response to the photographer qualified as true would dissolve, together with my presumably naïve trust in the power of green varnish. What the contextualist argument is exploiting are intuitions pertaining to the truth-values of certain utterances, in certain scenarios. Hence, what is important, together with a competent speaker's intuitions about 'the leaves' or 'is green', are the intuitively adequate assessments of the states of affairs with respect to which those utterances need to be evaluated.

The situation with the other examples in section 3 is similar. In all of these cases, it is one and the same condition that is being assessed. My utterances at the restaurant and at the ambassador's party both aim at describing the very same outfit: it simply is not part of the story that, as I left the restaurant and headed towards the embassy, I cut my tie, ripped my shirt, and rolled in mud. Similarly, my remarks about the baby carriage are both directed towards one and the same item, fixed in all of its relevant properties: as we interrupted our discussion of human dexterity and proceeded on our walk, we did not equip the stroller with larger tyres, headlights, and an internal combustion engine. But our intuitions regarding these cases are sensitive not only to the semantic profile of the uttered sentences and to the state of the objects being assessed. Knowledge of English and exhaustive information about how I was dressed that evening are insufficient for determining whether an utterance of 'My attire is formal' turns out as intuitively true or false. Linguistic competence and positive identification of the object you are pushing, though obviously necessary, are not enough for the assignment of one or another truth-value to utterances of 'This is a vehicle'. What is also required is a certain degree of familiarity with the purpose of the classification of attires as formal or informal, or of the decision of what qualifies as a vehicle on a given occasion. The friend who assured me that I would be welcome at the embassy was well acquainted with my jacket and tie, and knew that 'formal' meant, roughly, 'conforming to accepted rules or customs': he just did not know enough about the rules and customs commonly accepted within the diplomatic community. Those who, unlike my friend, correctly understand the inadequacy of my remark at the embassy, do so not only in virtue of their familiarity with the English idiom, and on the basis of what I was wearing that evening: their semantic appraisal is shaped, together with these undeniably relevant factors, by their understanding that, for the purpose of the ambassador's party, nothing less than a tuxedo qualifies as conforming to the accepted customs.

To put it otherwise: the kind of evidence acceptable in one scenario as relevant for the classification of a particular item as, say, a vehicle, pertaining among other things to that object's ability to efficiently transport people and goods, does not suffice for a similar categorization of that item with respect to the purpose of the other setting, where requirements of size and speed seem to play a more fundamental role. And the fact of the matter about my attire, such as that it included a tie and a double-breasted jacket, supports a conclusion in terms of formality from the point of view of restaurateurs unsympathetic to jeans and running shoes, but not from the perspective of diplomatic etiquette. By the same token, the type of evidence appropriate for the assessment of the colour of Pia's leaves when in discussion with a photographer pertains to the hue of their outermost surface: the leaves qualify as green as long as that surface is of a certain colour, that which we commonly label by means of the English expression 'green'. Shift to another scenario, such as the discussion with the botanist, and different demands are brought to the foreground, pertaining to the evidence required for a classification of certain objects as being of a particular colour. The procedure is now concerned with the discovery of the leaves' 'natural' tint—in our example, a procedure involving careful scraping of the paint, or study of photographs of the plant before the paint job. The leaves now count as green only as long as the appropriate items are of a certain colour, once again the colour we commonly denote by means of the English expression 'green'.

That, in the relevant sense, the leaves count as green on one occasion but not on the other is of course something the contextualists are at pains to stress, our intuitions regarding the truth-values of Pia's utterances resting precisely on the pretheoretic assessment of the leaves as green on one occasion, but not on the other. Travis, for instance, takes an explicit stance on this matter:

> The English 'is green' speaks of a certain way for things to be: green. One might say that it speaks of a certain property: (being) green. If we do say that, we must also say this about that property: what sometimes counts as a thing's having it sometimes does not. (Travis 1997: 98)

Recanati agrees:

> Insofar as 'red' refers to a specific colour (and it does) this, it seems, expresses a definite property... But in most cases the following question will arise: what is it for the thing talked about to count as having that colour?... To fix the utterance's truth-conditions, we need to know something more—something which the meanings of the words do not and cannot give us: we need to know what it is for that thing... to count as being that colour. (Recanati 2003: 96–7)

Carston, ironically in a section devoted precisely to the thesis that meaning underdetermines content, even goes as far as to talk of *the* proposition expressed by an utterance of 'This is green' (now applied to fruits with a green peel and white pulp), leaving the intuitive evaluations of the proposition as dependent upon the contextually appropriate choice of the relevant kind of evidence:

> [This case] may be judged true in a particular context provided its peel is green even though its interior is white and its stem is brown, while in a different circumstance (say, fruits are being separated into the ripe and the unripe), *the* proposition expressed will be evaluated according to whether or not the interior is green, the colour of the skin being irrelevant. (Carston 2002: 23–4, my italics)

Returning to Pia's case, then, the intuitive requirement it puts forth is that u, her utterance of 'The leaves are green' during the discussion with the photographer, be evaluated as true at particular points, those reflecting our assessment of the leaves as green. In the more austere jargon of the interpretive system, what needs to be obtained is a result of truth at points k such that, in k, the object denoted by [the leaves]$_{NP}$ partakes in the extension of [is green]$_{NP}$. Moreover, as far as our intuitions go, it is also desired that v, her utterance of 'The leaves are green' during the exchange with the botanist, turns out false at points of a different type, those corresponding to our understanding of the leaves as non-green. To put it otherwise: falsehood must be obtained whenever points k' are taken into consideration, such that the *denotatum* of [the leaves]$_{NP}$ is not a member of the value of [is green]$_{NP}$ at k'. This much, of course, is perfectly consistent with the results straightforwardly provided by traditional systems. For in their approach it is by no means surprising that an indexical-free clause (paired with any index i), when evaluated with respect to a certain point, ends up being associated with a truth-value distinct from that assigned to that very clause–index pair with respect to *another* point.[8]

So, the pre-theoretic assessment of the truth-conditions for the utterances under discussion constrains the interpretive system only in that it demands that such utterances be assigned truth with respect to points that give a positive reply to the query pertaining to the leaves' greenness; and that it yields a decision of falsity with respect to points in which the leaves do not participate in greenness. A demand of this kind does not amount to the requirement that the system assign distinct t-distributions to u and v: with respect to suitably distinct points of evaluation, one and the same t-distribution may naturally yield the desired truth-values. In other words, *pace* premiss (ii) in the argument responsible for the contextualists' excitement, it is not inevitably the case that utterances endowed with intuitively distinct truth-conditions are to be associated with distinct t-distributional profiles. Consequently, *pace* the contextualists (and the inadequate anti-contextualist replies considered in section 3), Pia's predicament is

---

[8] Recall that I am treating [the leaves]$_{NP}$ as a term denoting the appropriate foliage; nothing of importance hinges on this otherwise inadequate pretence.

compatible with an account grounded on plausible hypotheses of representation for her utterances, in turn evaluated along the lines suggested by straightforward interpretive systems.

5. *The Aims and Scope of Traditional Semantics*

Unlike the views criticized in section 3, my response to the contextualist challenge grants much to contextualism: in the sense of truth-conditions under discussion here—namely, truth-values with respect to particular conditions of the world—meaning does indeed fail to determine truth-conditions. Anyone caught by surprise by these conclusions has indeed reasons for regarding them as 'considerable', to echo Travis's first characterization of contextualism. Still, I remain highly sceptical with respect to the further connotation of 'exciting', at least when understood as an allusion to the rejection of an entrenched tradition in natural language semantics. To the contrary, at least once that tradition is properly understood, the examples put forth in the contextualist literature strike me as rather insipid: that colour-talk may be regulated along different lines in different contexts seems a relatively harmless thesis, one that should hardly alarm those operating within the traditional semantic paradigm. As far as the contextualists' examples go, contextual effects that are 'semantically relevant', in the sense of being in need of an explanation within the interpretive system, may well be limited to the type of contextuality explicitly steered by conventional meaning, i.e., indexicality. Contextual effects that are 'semantically relevant' in the sense that they play a role in the assignment of truth-conditions, on the other hand, unquestionably go beyond the meaning-controlled type of contextuality to which the system is attuned. But the fact that customary interpretive systems are not *sufficient* for the assignment of truth-conditions to an utterance is hardly surprising. On pretty much anyone's view, as I explained in Chapter 1, decisions of representation (such as those involving ambiguity resolution or ellipsis unpacking) remain out of the system's control, but are nevertheless obviously important for the assignment of truth-conditions to a given utterance. That the features relevant to those decisions, such as the speaker's intentions or the topic of conversation, may also come to play a role in the truth-conditional interpretation of the system's t-distributional verdict hardly seems to ruinously monkey-wrench the task for which traditional systems have been devised.

But my reply to the contextualists' polemical tone is unlikely to satisfy the traditionalists, unless an important worry is addressed explicitly. It may seem that, after all, my approach ends up throwing out the mainstream baby together with the contextualist bathwater: customary systems, so it may be objected, are preserved in their traditional form only at the cost of being deprived of any interesting contact with truth-conditions. Given that truth-conditions are precisely the sort of factors addressed by the relevant type of intuitions, so this objection concludes, granting all that I conceded to the contextualist cause risks depriving the mainstream approach of any empirical relevance. A conclusion of this type, so it seems, is reason enough for excitement—or despair, depending on one's sympathies.

This objection errs in presenting the picture from section 4 as the claim that interpretive systems have no contact with truth-conditions of the type relevant for our assessment of their empirical adequacy. It is true that some of our intuitions pertain to the truth-conditions of particular utterances on particular occasions, and that the interpretive system, unable to take into account a variety of contextual factors relevant in this respect, may not deliver results immediately comparable with them. But that truth-conditional conclusions do not depend solely upon the regularities encoded within the system does not entail that such regularities are of no truth-conditional relevance. A straightforward method for isolating the system's contribution to truth-conditions focuses on the *relationships* holding between particular sentences (clauses), once the parameters affecting the assignment of semantic properties to them are assumed to remain constant—or, by the same token, by investigating the semantic properties of certain sentences across all such parameters. In this way, the interpretive system is immediately responsible for *logical* verdicts—that is, truth-conditionally relevant conclusions amenable to intuitive assessment. I devote the final paragraphs of this chapter to a brief discussion of these conclusions, and of their significance with respect to the contextualist challenge.

It seems clear that a simple argument such as

(2) if there's cheese on the moon, then the moon is made of cheese,
there's cheese on the moon,
therefore, the moon is made of cheese

has a peculiar semantic profile: intuitively, and informally speaking, whenever the premisses provide a true description of how things happen to be with the moon, the conclusion does so as well. An intuition of this type seems unproblematically applicable to instances arguably involving ambiguity or ellipsis, such as

(3) if the moon is made of cheese, then Smith went to the bank,
the moon is made of cheese
therefore, Smith went to the bank,

or, for that matter,

(4) Smith went to the bank, therefore Smith went to the bank.

Uncontroversially, interpretive systems are unable to yield conclusions regarding the truth-conditions for utterances of the sentences occurring in (3) and (4): semantic results of any type may be obtained only with respect to the choice of appropriate clauses, such as a particular disambiguation of 'bank'. Yet, on pretty much anybody's view, interpretive systems bear an obvious responsibility with respect to a certain type of pre-theoretic, truth-conditionally relevant intuition. In particular, as long as 'bank' is used in one and the same sense, whenever the distribution of cheese in the solar system renders the premisses in (3) true, its conclusion also provides a true description of how things happen to be with Smith. In a more theoretically laden jargon, these intuitions of truth-conditions impose an obvious constraint on any system: given any fixed hypothesis regarding the clauses in the representations for the sentences in (3), these clauses must be such that, for any index i, the third of them is true with respect to i if the other two are. Though relatively straightforward, a requirement of this kind places non-trivial demands on the structure and content of the system.

When it comes to cases such as (3) and (4)—namely, cases involving disambiguation or other 'preparatory' matters—this conclusion is rather uncontroversial. The passage from Quine cited in Chapter 1 and repeated here already provides a clear indication of why, regardless of the 'magnitude of the applicational manœuvres' at issue, logical results are straightforwardly assessable.

Insofar as the interpretation of ambiguous expressions depends on circumstances of the argument as a whole—speaker, hearer, scene, date, and underlying problem and purpose—the fallacy of equivocation is not to be feared; for, those background circumstances may be expected to influence the interpretation of an ambiguous expression uniformly wherever the expression recurs in the course of the argument. (Quine 1953: 146)

A parallel response may be given to the objection I presented three paragraphs ago: namely, the complaint that, in my account, interpretive systems are improperly cut off from truth-conditional verdicts. Of course, at least according to the approach defended in this essay, the type of contextual dependence affecting cases such as Pia's utterances is dramatically different from the type of contextuality relevant to, say, the disambiguation of 'bank'. What is important for the purpose of this section, however, is the fact that, in either case, the system's inability to deliver truth-conditional results for particular utterances does not entail its indifference to *all* of our truth-conditionally significant intuitions. In particular, although the system alone, or even the system conjoined with certain hypotheses of disambiguation, remains unable to decide whether an utterance of

(1) The leaves are green

in a particular scenario is true or false, it is nevertheless committed to some conclusion or other pertaining to its interactions with other, suitably related instances. For instance, according to customary approaches, what emerges is that, if such an utterance on such an occasion provides a true description of how things happen to be, then the same must be the case for utterances of, say,

(5) Either the leaves are green or the moon is made of cheese

or

(6) If the moon is made of cheese, then the leaves are green

taking place in that very same scenario. Fix whatever parameters may eventually affect the truth-conditional interpretation of the system's outcome—in particular, fix any contextual factor that may affect your decisions regarding the colour of the leaves or the moon's composition. The relationships between (1) and (5) or (6) yielded by a particular interpretive system *do* entail significant and empirically testable hypotheses, at least pertaining to the expressions the system aims at analysing.

Interpretive systems are thus immediately responsible for outcomes of entailment, or for parallel results, such as the notion that, say, 'If the leaves are green, then the leaves are green' is logically true, that 'The leaves are green and the leaves are green' is redundant, and that 'The leaves are green and the leaves are not green' is contradictory. Considerations of this sort have always been the declared primary topic of contention for the empirical assessment of a semanticist's enterprise. Here is a typical example among many others from the introductory section of a traditional textbook: 'In constructing the semantic component of a grammar, we are attempting to account... for [speakers'] judgements of synonymy, entailment, contradiction, and so on' (Dowty *et al.* 1981: 2). A system suitably equipped to account for such judgements may well be unable to decide the colour of Pia's leaves, or to recommend what to wear when visiting the ambassador. Still, at least as far as the contextualist argument goes, its assessment of the relationships between meaning, truth, and the use of language remains on the right track.

6. *The Strange Story of Underarticulationism*

No discussion of the scope and significance of contemporary contextualism would be complete without explicit mention of the prototypical example of underarticulation: 'It is raining'. If I utter 'It is raining' in rainy Prague, my utterance is surely true; if I utter 'It is raining' in southern Spain, my utterance is unequivocally false. The point, contextualists insist, is the by now familiar one: given one unique meteorological condition of the world, utterances of one and the same non-ambiguous, non-indexical (tense aside) sentence end up with distinct truth-values.

The idea of underarticulation was brought to the attention of the philosophical community in an influential essay by John Perry (1986). The topic of Perry's essay is the possibility of a type of self-knowledge 'that requires no concept or idea of oneself', and, more generally, the possibility '[of having] information about something without having any "representation" of that thing' (Perry 1986: 138). The route leading Perry to these important remarks in the philosophy of mind begins with certain relatively harmless considerations about language, such as the denial of the principle that '[e]ach constituent of the proposition expressed by a statement is designated by a component of the statement' (Perry 1986: 140). From the semantic point of view, the brief discussion preceding this denial is marred by a nonchalant attitude towards concepts such as 'proposition', 'constituent', or 'aboutness', a nonchalance that is, on the other hand, not at all damaging from the point of view of Perry's agenda in the philosophy of mind. As for language, we are left with the not so contentious conclusion that

A use u of 'It is raining' expresses a proposition P, iff there are u', u'', u''', t, p, and R such that
 i) u' is a use of 'It'
 ii) u'' is a use of 'is' that designates t
 iii) u''' is a use of 'raining' that designates R
 iv) u occurs at p
 v) u consists of u' followed by u'' followed by u'''
 vi) P is the proposition that $R(p,t)$.
(Perry 1986: 141–2)

At least on a plausible understanding of the role that Perry's propositions are supposed to play, this amounts to the unsurprising conclusion that if you and I both utter 'It is raining', only you end up telling the truth if it rains where you are but not where I am. This unsurprising conclusion is quickly established in the first couple of pages: what matters, for Perry and for the reader, is not the point about rain, but what, at least according to Perry, is supposed to follow from it when it comes to questions of thought, representation, and the first person.[9]

The presumably semantically more alarming aspects of 'It is raining' seem to emerge in a later paper by Perry, co-authored with Mark Crimmins, even though they are relegated to the not so prominent, less than two-page-long, final section. There, after the discussion of certain views about beliefs and belief reports, Crimmins and Perry present rather unconventional conclusions about logic, semantics, and language, such as the notion that

there can be no simple logic of [belief reports]. The simplest possible rule,

$$\frac{A \text{ believes that } S}{A \text{ believes that } S}$$

does not hold in general. (Crimmins and Perry 1989: 710)

I'll return to the peculiarities of belief reports in the next chapter, where, among other things, I motivate my scepticism towards such an extreme conclusion (but not, it should be pointed out, towards much of what Perry and Crimmins say about beliefs, believing, and belief reports). Hints of the polemical tone in the last pages of Crimmins and Perry's 1989 paper occasionally reappear in Crimmins's book (Crimmins 1992b). Overall, however, Crimmins seems to be more interested in the consequences of underarticulationism with respect to belief reports than with the presumably controversial significance that this phenomenon may have for approaches grounded on standard interpretive systems. For instance, he notes that

it is always possible to hold that there is a covert syntactic expression that has as its content any propositional constituent whatever... In most of the counterexamples to full articulation, a posit of covert expressions will seem natural only on a way of drawing the distinction

---

[9] See also Perry 1998a and 1998b; Corazza 2003.

[between plausible and implausible posits of covert expressions] that is tied to semantic intuitions—intuitions that there is more to the truth conditions of uses of the expression in question than is overtly expressed. I have no particular objection to positing covert expressions for such reasons. (Crimmins 1992b: 16)

Regardless of Perry and Crimmins's true aims, the point of underarticulationism (and with the cognate notions of free enrichment, meaning underdetermination, and the like) is, in itself, rather harmless and unexciting. Of course, some utterances of 'It rains' turn out to be true and others false without intervening meteorological changes. Uncontroversially, what makes the difference between one occasion of speaking and another are contextual factors, such as the topic of conversation, the location of the speaker, the background information, or any other 'pragmatic' sort of phenomenon to which one may appeal. Typically, an utterance u of 'It rains' in rainy Prague aims at commenting on the local downpours, and is directed to an audience interested in whether they should pick up an umbrella. Clearly, in this context, neither Canadian snowstorms nor the Spanish drought play a relevant role as meteorological evidence of the type required: for present purposes, the actual condition is one in which it rains. Move to Catalunia, and the storm in Prague is likely not to qualify as relevant support for claims of rain: it is rain in Spain that is now required for the truth of an utterance of 'It is raining'. What exactly follows from this commonplace?

Let us suppose that you look at questions of language from afar: what you are satisfied with is the mere fact that, one way or another, utterances are assigned truth-conditions of a certain type. In this case, you are unlikely to be interested in many of the distinctions discussed in this essay: one way or another, for one reason or another, distinct utterances of 'It is raining' or 'The leaves are green' end up with different truth-conditional profiles, and the differences are, in one sense or another, questions of context. Suppose, then, that gazing from your distant viewpoint you ask: are there unarticulated constituents? Does meaning fail to determine truth-conditions? Do 'pragmatic' aspects of context make a difference to truth-value? I cannot see why anyone should strive to provide a negative reply to these questions. When considered from such a distance, of course, claims of underarticulation amount to nothing but verbal embellishments of the (correct) intuition that 'It is raining' may be uttered truly at a rainy place, but not wherever the sun is shining. In this vague and distant sense, of course, it is hardly an axiom of mainstream semantics that things ought to be otherwise. Distance should not be underestimated: interesting philosophical conclusions may well be drawn from a remote viewpoint, Perry's original essay (1986) being a case in point. From a semantic point of view, however, and in particular from the point of view of an assessment of traditional interpretive systems, a much closer look is required.

Suppose, then, that you are interested in the inner workings of the processes leading to the interpretation of particular utterances, in the different ways in which context may intervene, and in the ways in which the system's mechanisms may come in to play. Suppose, in other words, that you are interested in theories of meaning, truth, and the use of language, such as the view that has emerged from the first chapters of this book. Then there emerges a sense in which meaning does determine a distribution of truth-values across distinct parameters. But in this sense, nothing in the aforementioned commonsensical conclusions about the weather appears to be at all problematic: nothing in the everyday use and evaluation of 'It rains' lends support to a conclusion in terms of alternative t-distributions.[10] What the evidence at hand indicates is the need for a conclusion of

---

[10] On underarticulation see e.g. Perry 1986; Crimmins and Perry 1989; Crimmins 1992b, 1995; Recanati 1993, 2002; and Taylor 2001.

differing truth-conditions, given fixed assumptions of meaning. And in this sense, once again, nothing worrisome seems to arise for traditional interpretive systems: the analysis of meaning and t-distributions they yield is not at all incompatible with the needed truth-conditional outcomes.[11]

7. *Where Am I Now?*

The main aim of this chapter has been to defend traditional interpretive systems, such as that sketched in Chapter 1, from criticisms emerging from contextualist quarters. At the core of my response lie distinctions of central importance for the assessment of the system's relationship with particular utterances, and with our semantic intuitions about them. In particular, I explained why the system yields conclusions of t-distributions, and I discussed the interface between such conclusions and our intuitions of truth-conditions. In section 5, I paused on the significance of systems geared towards results of this type. Although they are related to actual instances of language use only via the mediation of suitable additional hypotheses, these structures put forth important and informative (or mis-informative, depending on the route they decide to take) claims pertaining to the meaning of particular expressions, and to the relationships they bear to issues of truth-value.

But it is not only contextualists who have been targeted in this chapter. As I explained, an adequate assessment of the role and scope of traditional systems also reveals the inadequacy of a variety of anti-contextualist strategies that have recently been developed in traditionalist quarters. In this chapter, as in the chapters that preceded it, I did not intend to take sides on debates

---

[11] For a more detailed application of this chapter's strategy to 'It rains', see my Predelli, forthcoming.

apparently grounded on faulty premisses: inadequate defences of the theoretical viewpoint to which I am sympathetic need not be received with a lenient attitude, because that viewpoint may be grounded on a much more solid foundation. This attitude also motivates my next chapter, where I address a debate internal to the traditional approach to semantic matters, but possibly vitiated by some erroneous assumptions regarding the interpretive system's approach to meaning and truth.

Chapter 5
The Easy Problem of Belief Reports

In the previous chapters, I focused on the traditional understanding of meaning and truth, and on the relationship between the interpretive system's mechanisms and particular instances involving the use of language. My strategy was grounded on the distinction between, on the one hand, the system's aims and scope, and, on the other hand, the items with respect to which its result may eventually be compared. In particular, I stressed that our pre-theoretic semantic judgements focus on the truth-conditions of particular utterances, but that systems do not take utterances into consideration, and do not yield immediate truth-conditional conclusions about them. The analysis of the relationships between the system's inputs—namely clause–index pairs—and particular utterances has been the topic of Chapters 2 and 3. In Chapter 4, I turned to a discussion of the system's output, and to a discussion of the interface between conclusions of t-distributions and results of truth-conditions.

In Chapter 4 I was primarily concerned with a defence of the traditional approach to semantics against the contextualist attack. Although the contextualist research project may well unveil a variety of interesting aspects of the processes of communication or understanding, its criticism of mainstream semantics derives from an important misunderstanding of the theory of meaning and truth upon which it is grounded. Still, such a misunderstanding is to a certain extent comprehensible: as I explained, even some among the prominent defenders of the traditional stance have assumed an inadequate view of truth and meaning, distinct from the account to which their approach is in fact committed.

It should come as no surprise, then, that discussions *internal* to the traditional research programme end up being vitiated by an incorrect appreciation of certain fundamental features of the interpretive system's procedures. As a result of a more appropriate understanding of these issues, some of the perennial semantic puzzles discussed within the customary paradigm may in fact turn out to be more easily approachable than is commonly assumed, at least when it comes to the structure and content of interpretive systems suited to their analysis. In this chapter, I substantiate this claim by focusing on one of the prototypical sources of befuddlement for mainstream philosophical semanticists: namely, the behaviour of singular terms (in particular, proper names) within attitude reports.

According to widespread consensus, the analysis of sentences such as 'Tom believes that Bush is the President' yields central and unexpected conclusions about the semantic profile of this or that expression, or about the reliability of our semantic intuitions. For some, any correct treatment of those locutions must end up recognizing surprising aspects to the behaviour of proper names such as 'Bush', over and above their ability to pick out a particular individual.[1] According to others, the analysis of belief reports unveils otherwise unsuspected sources of indexicality, in

---

[1] For different versions of this stance, see e.g. Frege 1892; Forbes 1990 and 1993. For comments on Forbes, see Crimmins 1993.

particular with respect to 'believes' or 'that'.[2] As hinted in the final section of Chapter 4, some think that languages equipped with the resources of propositional attitude attributions stretch the applicability of traditional logical structures, and reveal the unsoundness of inference rules as prima facie obvious as the rule of repetition.[3] Last, but not least, an influential movement counters that the study of our descriptions of Tom's cognitive predicament uncovers competent speakers' unreliability in providing semantically dependable judgements of content and/or truth-value.[4]

It is not my intention in this chapter to counter any of these claims. Perhaps names do have a Fregean *Sinn*, and perhaps some prima-facie obvious inference rules may turn out not to be inference rules at all. Possibly, competent speakers sometimes get things wrong, and in all likelihood there are more indexicals under the sun than the obvious ones I considered in Chapter 1. But, so I claim, no support for such relatively unexpected, philosophically strong conclusions is to be obtained from the analysis of the semantic behaviour of attitude reports. My strategy in favour of this conclusion goes as follows. I *assume* the denial of all of the controversial conclusions allegedly entailed by the study of belief reports; that is, I rest satisfied with certain straightforward hypotheses about names, attitude predicates, and semantic intuitions. I then explain how interpretive systems grounded on these naïve assumptions may reach the correct conclusions

---

[2] For a sophisticated treatment of attitude predicates along indexical lines, see Richard 1990b, 1993, and 1995. See also Schiffer 1990, 1992, and 1996. For comments and criticisms, see Crimmins 1992a; Ludlow 1995 and 1996; Reimer 1995; Sider 1995.

[3] See Crimmins and Perry 1989; Crimmins 1992b and 1995. For criticisms see Clapp 1995 and Saul 1993. For an interesting alternative take on belief reports, see Santambrogio 2002.

[4] For distinct versions of this suggestion, see Berg 1988; Braun 1998; Salmon 1986, 1989, 1991, and 1995; Soames 1987a, 1987b, and 1995. See also Wettstein 1986.

pertaining to attitude reports, provided that such conclusions are understood in the light of the results reached in Chapter 4.

1. *A Simple System*

In Chapter 1, I provided a sketchy presentation of an impoverished fragment of English, accompanied by a relatively simple semantic analysis of the expressions it contains. Given the aim of the first chapters in this book—namely, to discuss general questions pertaining to the system's understanding of meaning and truth—I could afford to be relatively non-committal with respect to a variety of otherwise important questions pertaining to this or that expression. However, when it comes to the topic of this chapter, a closer look at the locutions occurring in my central examples cannot be avoided. I will thus have to say something about the system's treatment of, for instance, 'believes', 'that', 'Bush', 'that Bush is the President', and 'Tom believes that Bush is the President'. Still, my central aim here is not to provide an analysis of these expressions, but rather to dissolve the 'classic problems' they appear to generate, such as apparent failures of substitutivity of co-referential names within embedded clauses. In order to show that these problems are, in this respect, 'easy' ones, I put forth exceedingly simple-minded, widely known theses pertaining to proper names, complementizers, and attitude predicates. I then explain how, granting no more exotic resources than these assumptions, a satisfactory treatment of attitude reports is available, on the basis of the customary resources offered by traditional interpretive systems.

Let us begin with belief reports such as

(1) Tom believes that Bush is the President.

It seems reasonable to suppose that their rough semantic interpretation ought to proceed along relational lines: a certain binary cognitive relation is alleged to hold between Tom and something else. The choice of the appropriate relation, of course, must depend upon the semantic contribution offered by 'believes'. In the absence of arguments to the contrary, and leaving aside questions of tense, it also seems that such a contribution remains invariant across indexes—that is, in the vocabulary from Chapter 1, that 'believes' is associated with a constant character. Let us now suppose that the *relatum* involved (together with Tom) in the relationship provided by 'believes' is semantically supplied by the 'that'-clause, in this case 'that Bush is the President'. Given this much, it seems plausible at least initially to hypothesize that the contribution of the 'that' clause depends solely upon the structure and composition of the embedded clause, in the case of (1) the sentence 'Bush is the President'.

According to a simple development of the suggestions in the foregoing paragraph, the semantic role played by a 'that'-clause may be represented by means of an n-tuple containing the contributions offered by the expressions within the embedded sentence. Ignoring a few not immediately relevant complications, the semantic interpretation of 'that Bush is the President' (with respect to an index i) may thus be rendered by means of a set-theoretic structure such as

<semantic contribution of 'Bush' in i, semantic contribution of 'is the President' in i>.

It is obvious that the choice of such structures also depends upon the conventions adopted in the theory's metalanguage, such as the notion that the semantic value of 'Bush' comes first, and the contribution of the predicate comes second. There are of course no significant theoretical decisions involved in the preference for the aforementioned n-tuple over, say,

<semantic contribution of 'is the President' in i, semantic contribution of 'Bush' in i>

as long as one proceeds in a consistent manner. As for this *n*-tuple's components, the decision pertaining to what 'is the President' supplies is a question that plays no role in the debate under discussion. For concreteness' sake, I assume that, with respect to any index *i*, what is at issue is a certain property, *presidency*. More immediately relevant is the question of the contribution offered by 'Bush' with respect to an index *i*. Assume, then, what I take to be the most straightforward suggestion that one can come up with in this respect: the contribution offered by a proper name with respect to any index is the name's referent.[5] It follows that, taking the aforementioned hypotheses for granted, the contribution offered by 'that Bush is the President' with respect to any index is representable as the pair

$C = $ <Bush, presidency>.

Put together all of the above, and grant a few harmless additional assumptions. What you get is a result pertaining to the t-distribution for (1) with respect to an index *i*. Given the clause–index pair <(1), *i*>, consisting of (a clause appropriate for) (1) and an index *i*, it follows from interpretive systems grounded on the foregoing hypotheses that

<(1), *i*> is true with respect to a point *k* iff the pair <Tom, *C*> belongs in the extension of 'believes' at *k*.

Clearly, the same t-distribution is also assigned to other clause–index pairs. To begin with, given that 'Dubya' is co-referential with 'Bush', it is an immediate consequence of the aforementioned hypotheses that the report

(2) Tom believes that Dubya is the President,

---

[5] This assumption is consistent with what is often called 'Millianism', a natural offspring of the so-called *direct reference* movement (see the classic Kripke 1972 and Kaplan 1977, and the discussion in Marti 2003); for a general presentation and defence of Millianism, see Salmon 1986. For a view of proper names as indexicals, see Recanati 1993; for a criticism, see Predelli 2001.

paired with the index i, is associated with the same t-distribution to which the system maps $<(1), i>$. Moreover, on the assumption that proper names have a constant character, and that the only index-sensitive elements involved in the other expressions in (1) are the verbal tenses, it follows that the only parameter relevant to the interpretation of indexical expressions is the index's temporal co-ordinate. Thus, given any index j that agrees with i as to its temporal co-ordinate, the pair consisting of (1) and j is associated with the t-distribution appropriate for $<(1), i>$. These consequences deserve to be labelled for further reference:

(i) identical t-distributions are assigned to the sentence-indexes $<(1), i>$ and $<(2), i>$, for any index i,

and

(ii) identical t-distributions are assigned to the sentence-indexes $<(2), i>$ and $<(2), j>$, for any indexes i and j that do not differ in their temporal parameter.

These conclusions are important, because they are typically taken to entail the incompatibility of the simple-minded system I proposed with certain intuitions about utterances of sentences such as (1) and (2). It is to the discussion of the interface between (i) and (ii) and these intuitions that I turn in the next section.

It may be worth repeating that my quick presentation of some views on names, attitude predicates, and the like is not at all intended to provide arguments in their favour. In fact, the point is not even that of proposing prima-facie correct assumptions, worthy of being upheld in the absence of arguments to the contrary. As far as I am concerned, there may well be important counter-arguments to my Millian take on names, against the binary reading of 'believes', or against any of the other hypotheses I envisioned. Still, if this chapter is on the right track, one very prominent argumentative strategy against the simple

The Easy Problem of Belief Reports ~ 167

system outlined in this section is not convincing. More importantly from this essay's point of view, as I explain in section 4, the reason for its failure has to do with a fundamental misunderstanding of the role which systems are supposed to play, and of the relationships between their outcomes and our truth-conditional intuitions.

2. Tom's Predicament

As explained in the previous chapters, the hypotheses and results of an interpretive system need to be tested for empirical adequacy; i.e., they need to be compared with competent speakers' pre-theoretic reactions. Such reactions, or at least those that are of interest for the purpose of this essay, pertain to the truth-conditions of particular *utterances*.

Consider, then, the case of Tom, who does not know that 'Bush' and 'Dubya' are two names for the same man. Tom, a competent and reflective English speaker, sincerely assents to 'Bush is the President', but has no inclination to assent to 'Dubya is the President'.[6] Tom's case is of interest from this chapter's point of view, for at least two reasons. First, on some occasions, Tom's ignorance of these names' co-referentiality seems to matter when reporting on his beliefs. For instance, I may explain Tom's indifference to your exclamation of 'There goes Dubya' by commenting: 'He does not know that Dubya is the President'. In this scenario (*scenario A*, for further reference) an utterance u_1 of

(1) Tom believes that Bush is the President

seems true, but an utterance u_2 of

(2) Tom believes that Dubya is the President

[6] For a discussion of the appropriate caveats see Kripke 1979.

appears to be false. Secondly, in other settings, Tom's attitudes towards Bush's appellations seem irrelevant. So, if you and I are accustomed to referring to Bush as 'Dubya', I may well comment on Tom's view of the President as a conservative by telling you 'Tom thinks that all Presidents are conservative, and he knows that Dubya is one of them'. In this setting (hereafter *scenario B*), an utterance u_3 of (2) seems entirely acceptable.

What the case of Tom elicits are relatively firm intuitions regarding the apparent truth-conditions for certain utterances. Since u_1 strikes us as true, but u_2 appears to be false, and since both aim at providing a description of one and the same cognitive situation of Tom's, u_1 and u_2 have apparently distinct truth-conditions; similar considerations hold for u_2 and u_3. What remains to be assessed is the significance of reactions of this type with respect to the results required of adequate interpretive systems. As I explained in Chapter 1, given the assumption that a certain clause (say, the uttered sentence, or a suitably related construct) and index are appropriate for a given utterance u, it is possible to interpret a system's results as the assignment of a t-distribution to u itself: the system assigns to u the t-distribution to which the clause–index pair in question is mapped. When it comes to the aforementioned utterances of (1) and (2), it seems clear that no distinctions of temporal co-ordinates are of relevance, since we may well imagine them taking place at roughly the same time. It follows that u_1 and u_2, the utterances of (1) and (2) in scenario A, receive the t-distributional profile associated with, respectively, the pairs <(1), i> and <(2), i>, for the appropriate index i. Similarly, it appears that u_1 and u_3, the utterances of (2) in the alternative scenario, involve one and the same clause, and indexes that do not differ in their temporal co-ordinates.

Given such hypotheses, and given (i) and (ii) above, it follows that the simple system from section 1 ends up associating the same t-distribution to all three utterances: at any point of evaluation, u_1, u_2, and u_3 share their truth-value. And this, so the story goes, won't do, at least as long as our intuitions of contrasting truth-conditions are taken seriously.

3. The Role of Context

A closer look at Tom's predicament and at our intuitions may be in order at this stage. Still, what matters for the purpose of this chapter is nothing more sophisticated than a relatively simple description of some aspects of Tom's cognitive profile, and of certain contextual features responsible for our reactions with respect to this or that report. What follows, in other words, is to a large extent a mere description of (part of) the *explanandum*, one that may be welcome to semanticists of very different orientations. What is important from my point of view is not how the sketchy comments I propose may be developed into persuasive theories in philosophical psychology or in the theory of communication, but how the background they depict may be appropriately accounted for within a systematic theory of semantic interpretation.

Modulo some not immediately relevant differences, there appears to be widespread agreement that what is at issue in Tom's story are his contrasting dispositions towards Bush's presidency, roughly depending upon appropriate *relata* involved in his cognitive attitudes. Let us say, then, that Tom is suitably disposed towards the information pertaining to Bush and his presidency when such information is presented to him in a 'normal' manner, say, by means of televised pictures of Bush during his presidential moments, or by means of sentences such as 'Bush is the President'.[7] Let us also agree that he is not so disposed towards that information when it is presented to him by means of other kinds

---

[7] For a discussion of 'normality' (phrased in the jargon of concrete, particular mental states), see Crimmins 1992b.

of items, such as sentences involving the name 'Dubya'. (In a fashionable theoretically laden presentation of this account, what matters is whether Tom is in a suitable triadic cognitive relation towards that piece of information with respect to some appropriate 'mode of presentation'.) Moreover, again *modulo* a variety of details that are not crucial for my purpose, one or another of the *relata* apparently involved in Tom's cognitive relationship to Bush's presidency seems to be contextually salient in a given scenario. For one reason or another, when discussing Tom's views in contexts of a particular type, 'normal' presentations of Bush are of special prominence. In contexts of a different type, however, what somehow manages to come to the foreground are Tom's relations towards Bush and his being the President mediated by less customary *relata*, such as presentations of Bush as the man nicknamed 'Dubya'.

Let us then settle for a rough-and-ready description of the contextual backgrounds relevant for the cases involving the utterances of (1) and (2) from section 2. Recall scenario B, in which conversants accustomed to the use of 'Dubya' as a name for Bush assess Tom's view of the President as a conservative. In this setting, what is important, in virtue of factors such as the conversants' interests or the focus of the conversation, is whether Tom is favourably related to the information that Bush is the President when it is presented to him in the normal way: what matters is roughly whether Tom is among those who assent to 'Bush is the President', or who sincerely utter 'He is the President' when pointing at the man in the Oval Office. The case is importantly different in scenario A, where what is at issue is an explanation of Tom's indifference to your exclamation of 'There goes Dubya'. What is now relevant, again in virtue of elements such as the point of our conversational exchange, is whether Tom is positively inclined towards the claim that Bush is the President when that claim is presented to him by means of appropriate linguistic devices. In a setting of this kind, focused on the choice between particular names, the *use* of an expression may contribute to raising it to contextual salience, along the lines of a pragmatic mechanism briefly discussed in Chapter 3. As I explained in my discussion of cases such as Quine's 'Giorgione' example and that of 'rhinoceros', there seems to be relatively firm support for what I called the *Verbal Salience Thesis*: namely, the claim that

> utterances of an expression *e* in a suitable context *c* may contribute to rendering *e* salient in *c*.

Scenario A is apparently a context of this type. Given that we are now interested in Tom's cognitive attitudes *vis-à-vis* particular appellations for Bush, the very wording we choose to express our views on Tom's cognitive life presumably contributes to raising to salience expressions of an appropriate kind. So, in this approach, an utterance u_2 of (2) in scenario A is to be evaluated with respect to a background in which what is relevant is Tom's disposition towards sentences such as 'Dubya is the President'. In the very same scenario—that is, in a setting in which we are sensitive to Tom's reactions *vis-à-vis* the President's names— utterances of (1) contribute to raising to salience *relata* of a different kind, roughly those involving Bush's more customary appellation.[8]

It is undeniable that the foregoing passages leave many questions unaddressed. What is desirable, for one thing, is a more accurate and detailed explanation of what 'modes of presentation' are, of how they are to be individuated, and of the role they play in our cognitive lives. For another, it would be of interest from the point of view of a theory of communication to discuss in a more rigorous manner the mechanisms responsible for the

---

[8] The relationships between the use of a name and the constraints on the appropriate media on particular occasions is by no means inevitably as simple. For a discussion of a variety of difficult cases, and for a promising suggestion as to their analysis, see in particular Saul 1998.

'contextual salience' to which I repeatedly alluded. Yet, that such issues in pragmatics and cognitive psychology are not analysed here in greater detail does not entail that the picture presented thus far is of no use for the solution of the semantic puzzle raised by utterances of belief reports. Conversely, and more interestingly from my point of view, acceptance of something along the foregoing lines by no means suffices for particular conclusions in this latter respect: general agreement on the rough sketch I put forth does not trickle down to a parallel degree of concordance when it comes to the semantic profile of sentences such as (1) and (2). This much should come as no surprise at this stage. As indicated in the previous chapters, agreement on at least the general traits of the contextual sensitivity apparently affecting the use and understanding of natural languages is compatible with very different approaches to how such sensitivity ought to be reflected within a suitable semantic theory.

At the end of section 2, the discussion of cases such as (1) and (2) led to the widespread conviction that the simple system from section 1 could not cope with the evidence supplied by our pre-theoretic intuitions of truth-value. On the basis of this assumption, the following dilemma is inevitable: either one relinquishes at least some of the assumptions taken for granted by that system, or one finds a good reason for not taking pre-theoretic intuitions at face value. According to the first horn of the dilemma, sufficiently sophisticated views of proper names, attitude predicates, and complementizers should be developed, so as to render the system appropriately receptive to the aforementioned differences between conversational settings such as scenarios A and B. According to the second horn, our truth-conditional intuitions ought to be relinquished as unreliable, and as unduly attentive to contextual peculiarities relevant at some appropriate level (for example, at the level of so-called speaker's meaning), but idle with respect to an utterance's strict truth-conditional profile. In what follows, I argue that the assumption giving rise to this dilemma is incorrect. The system from section 1, so I explain, is in fact compatible with the intuitive truth-conditional profile of cases such as u_1, u_2, and u_3, given the understanding of contextual sensitivity developed in Chapter 4.

4. Intuitions and Interpretive Systems

As I explained in the previous chapters, interpretive systems map utterances to t-distributions: that is, to functions from points of evaluation to truth-values. A point of evaluation is the kind of object that provides a definite answer to questions such as those pertaining to the extensions of predicates, the denotations of definite descriptions, or the truth-values of sentences (with respect to an index). Such results may eventually be compared with our pre-theoretic intuitions, or, at least, with those that are deemed to be worthy of the semanticist's attention. These intuitions put forth relatively firm claims pertaining to the truth-value of an utterance, given certain particular (actual or imaginary) worldly conditions; that is, in a more widespread terminology, they put forth decisions regarding its truth-conditions. So, what is required of an intuitively satisfactory interpretive system is that the t-distribution it assigns to an utterance v bears a satisfactory relation to our intuitions about v's truth-conditions.

In Chapter 4 I argued that this comparison is not immediate. As a reminder of the issues involved in this respect (entirely independent from issues of belief reports), consider yet another example from the contextualist camp, this time borrowed from John Searle (1980). Take the sentence

(3) Bill cut the grass,

and a situation in which Bill employed a pair of scissors to separate each of the grass blades along their vertical axis. Imagine now an utterance v of (3), taking place during a discussion pertaining to whether Bill mowed the lawn. In a scenario of this kind, at least if our pre-theoretic inclinations are to be trusted, v is false: Bill's actions do not count as cutting the grass, because, given the purpose at hand, cutting the grass involves shortening the blades by virtue of slicing them along a direction roughly parallel to the ground. But consider a less common setting, in which, due to superstitions regarding the number of grass blades in one's garden, Bill's employer demands that it be doubled by parting each leaflet in two. Take now an utterance v' of (3) in a setting of this kind; in this case, the situation at hand seems to qualify as a worldly condition with respect to which v' is true.

So, v and v'—that is, utterances of (3) taking place in the aforementioned settings—intuitively differ in truth-value, even if evaluated with respect to one and the same worldly condition, one in which Bill separates the grass blades with the help of a pair of scissors. What is a pre theoretically adequate interpretive system to do with respect to such evidence of different truth-conditions? Faced with this question, one may perhaps conclude that 'cut' must have been employed ambiguously, or that it indexically picks up distinct properties with respect to a contextually provided 'direction of incision'. Philosophers well disposed towards the notion of underarticulation may suggest that, appearances notwithstanding, 'cut' is semantically associated with a *triadic* relation, holding between a cutter, a cuttee, and a (typically unarticulated) 'purpose of separation'. Others, less sympathetic to unexpected appeals to indexicality or underarticulation, may deny that our initial assessments of truth-value are worthy of semantic recognition, and may suggest that they be analysed in terms of pragmatically conveyed information involving the aforementioned triadic relation: Bill, the grass, and alternative ways of cutting.

Still, in light of the variety of examples discussed in Chapter 4, I take it to be clear that solutions tailored to the case of 'cut' and/or the analysis of the cutting-relation do not provide a satisfactory solution to the *general* problem raised by examples such as (3). More importantly, none of these rather unorthodox and at least prima-facie surprising moves seems warranted by the cases under discussion. Take Bill's story again. As Searle correctly points out, our intuitions regarding utterances of (3) differ 'not because of the different *semantic* content [of "cut" or "grass"], nor because of any vagueness in the original, but because I know a lot of things about grass' (Searle 1980: 227). I know, in particular, a few things about grass and the act of cutting it: I know that, for everyday purposes, Bill's actions do not count as cutting the grass, but that, for the unusual requirement of the other scenario, they do. In a more epistemologically oriented jargon: I know that what qualifies as evidence for grass cutting on one occasion, the shortening of the blades by means of horizontal incisions, does not so qualify for the purpose of the other scenario. It is precisely such a difference between our interpretations of how things stand with Bill and the grass that apparently motivates our inclinations pertaining to the truth-values of the utterances in question. For instance, on occasions when Bill's actions do not count as having cut the grass, utterances stating otherwise turn out to be false; in settings in which what he did qualifies as an instance of grass cutting, utterances saying that he did cut the grass turn out, unsurprisingly, to be true.

This intuitively plausible informal assessment of Searle's example provides important indications regarding the interface between truth-conditions and t-distributions. As I stressed, when an interpretive system is applied to the sentence–index pair appropriate to a particular utterance, it yields verdicts in terms of t-distributions—that is, truth-values at points of evaluation. Yet, although both utterances v and v' of (3) take place *vis-à-vis* a state of affairs in which Bill vertically severs the leaflets, it is a different understanding of Bill's relation to the grass that motivates our inclination to judge one utterance, but not the other, as true. Given that our intuitions of truth-value are grounded, among other things, on different interpretations of the situation at hand, the constraint which such intuitions impose on any satisfactory analysis of v and v' must appropriately reflect this discrepancy. In other words, if our intuitions are to be reflected within the system in an adequate manner, what is needed is that the intuitively correct truth-values be obtained with respect to points mirroring the interpretations of Bill's actions appropriate for the settings in which each utterance takes place: in the case of v, a verdict of falsehood with respect to any point at which Bill is not a member of the extension of 'cut the grass', and, in the case of v', a verdict of truth with respect to any point at which he is. A requirement of this kind, of course, does not warrant a conclusion in terms of distinct t-distributions: that is, the conclusion that any adequate module should map v to a truth-value t at some point k, and v' to a distinct truth-value t' at that very point.

If this assessment of the story of Bill (and of the anecdotes in Chapter 4, involving the use of 'is green', 'is formal', or 'is a vehicle') is on the right track, then premisses of truth-conditional discrepancy do not entail the conclusion that empirically adequate systems should yield correspondingly different t-distributional outcomes. Utterances such as v and v' do indeed have different truth-conditions, in that they put forth contrasting demands regarding the worldly conditions needed for truth. It does not follow, however, that they ought to be interpreted by appealing to different t-distributions, and that improbable claims of indexicality or underarticulation provide the only alternative to a distrustful attitude towards our inclinations.

What do superstitious lawn owners have to do with the case of Tom's beliefs? The discussion of v and v' has brought to light the independent inadequacy of the prima-facie unobjectionable methodology I called the 'snapshot strategy', leading from intuitions of truth-conditional differences to results in terms of alternative t-distributions. But it is precisely a strategy of this kind that implicitly supports the widespread consensus regarding what any interpretive system for

(1) Tom believes that Bush is the President

and

(2) Tom believes that Dubya is the President

needs to explain, as long as our intuitions are deemed to be worthy of semantic recognition. Freeze Tom's cognitive life, so the story goes, and allow for neither changes of mind nor the acquisition of new beliefs. Since u_1 and u_2, and u_2 and u_3 differ intuitively in truth-value with respect to the way things are with Tom, so it is typically concluded, empirically adequate systems must map these utterances to suitably different t-distributions, unless an explanation is offered as to why our pre-theoretic evaluations systematically yield wrong results.

Yet, it is not only the case that the snapshot strategy is not *generally* applicable, as testified by the example of Bill and by the cases in Chapter 4. It seems also plausible to conclude that instances involving the categorization of an agent's cognitive profile, such as the scenarios involving (1) and (2), are no less 'occasion-sensitive' than the classification of certain events as cutting-events, or the appraisal of certain items of clothing as formal. Competent, intelligent English speakers are not only proficient with the use of expressions such as 'cut', 'is formal', or 'believes that Bush is the President'. They are also sufficiently attuned to the purposes and aims regulating the intuitively appropriate interpretation of certain states of affairs on particular occasions as instances of cutting, cases of formality, or examples of bearing a favourable attitude towards Bush's presidency.

Take scenario B, and consider an intuitively appropriate assessment of Tom's attitudes towards C, the claim pertaining to Bush and his presidency. Is Tom favourably related to C, for all purposes relevant on this occasion? As hinted in section 3, given the point of such inquiry, eventually having to do with Tom's political stance, the answer must apparently be positive: for instance, Tom sincerely assents to appropriate sentences expressing C, which he fully and correctly understands. For all relevant purposes, in other words, Tom's demeanour may well be accepted as sufficient evidence of his being appropriately related to C, in the manner apparently sanctioned by (1). In a more revealing terminology, the points of evaluation suitably reflecting Tom's state of mind are on this occasion points k such that in k' Tom and C are related in the belief way. Shift to scenario A, and Tom's willingness to assent to some but not all sentences encoding C becomes important as evidence justifying the categorization of his cognitive life. In particular, in the setting for u_1, in which what come into the foreground are expressions involving the name 'Bush', what is required is that Tom be appropriately related to C when it is presented to him by means of sentences such as 'Bush is the President'. But in the setting for u_2, where what is salient are locutions involving 'Dubya', what is needed is that Tom and C be suitably related with respect to expressions involving that name. Thus, given how things stand with Tom, this latter case is one which, for all relevant purposes, corresponds to a point of evaluation k' such that in k' Tom and C do not belong in the extension for 'believes'.

Given that our intuitions regarding u_1, u_2, and u_3 are also shaped by suitably differing inclinations regarding who believes what, an adequate interpretive system is required to yield the correct truth-values with respect to the points appropriately reflecting those inclinations. Recall, then, the interpretive system from section 1, committed to conclusions such as

(i) identical t-distributions are assigned to the sentence–indexes $<(1), i>$ and $<(2), i>$, for any index i,

and

(ii) identical t-distributions are assigned to the sentence–indexes <(2), i> and <(2), j>, for any indexes i and j that do not differ in their temporal parameter.

When coupled with the obvious hypotheses of representation for u_1, u_2, and u_3, that system is not only not prevented from satisfying the aforementioned *desideratum*, but it does in fact straightforwardly obey it. At least on the basis of the views on contextual salience defended here, the intuitions that govern our approach to the truth-conditions for u_1, u_2, and u_3 are as easily accommodated as our pre-theoretic assessment of my comments on Bill's actions or of your remarks on my suit.

5. Much Ado About Nothing?

Why does any of this matter? The point, as I stressed at the beginning of this chapter, is not to present a novel theory of belief reports. To the contrary, it is part and parcel of my dialectical strategy that none of the hypotheses embedded within my analysis of u_1, u_2, and u_3 is at all new or original. The aim of this chapter, rather, is to assess the demands that attitude reports make on empirically adequate interpretive systems. Against common consensus, I concluded that such demands are quite inconsequential: even the conjunction of the most straightforward and widely known theses about proper names, attitude predicates, and the like, yields outcomes compatible with our intuitive assessments of truth-conditions.

This conclusion does not amount to a defence of the simple-minded approach of section 1. In particular, as far as this chapter goes, a variety of *independent* arguments may well be mounted against the view of names as mere referential devices, against the interpretation of attitude predicates along binary, non-indexical lines, or against the reliability of competent speakers' truth-conditional intuitions. What matters from my point of view is a twofold methodological conclusion: the phenomenon highlighted by 'Bush'/'Dubya' type of examples is easily explainable within customary interpretive systems equipped only with straightforward hypotheses, and the widespread conviction to the contrary is grounded on the equally widespread misunderstanding of the system's approach to meaning, truth, and the use of language.

The disclaimer at the beginning of this section deserves to be repeated. In particular, what I should address are rejoinders along the lines of 'Ah, but this is just the same view as (equivalent to, a mere verbal embellishment of)...'—with the dots filled in by allusions to some well-known and ingenious theory, typically either the pragmatic take possibly championed by Nathan Salmon and Scott Soames or the underarticulationist line developed by Mark Crimmins and John Perry. I am thankful for the association of my sketchy remarks on attitude reports with such well-developed, interesting accounts, and I am by no means concerned about the objection that my approach to belief reports merely reflects already well-established theories. Indeed, when it comes to the analysis of the contributions provided by 'believes', 'that'-clauses, and proper names, the view considered in section 1 is by and large in agreement with the theory put forth, for instance, by Salmon (1986). If Salmon's allusion to systematically mistaken truth-conditional intuitions is abandoned in favour of my distinction between t-distributions and truth-conditions, the resulting position may indeed correspond to the view I defended: the judgements offered by competent speakers do not constrain the system in such a manner that utterances such as u_1 and u_2 need be associated with different truth-values at some unique point of evaluation. Similarly, in my view, as in the proposal of Crimmins and Perry (1989), the truth-value of an utterance of a belief report depends upon contextual elements that are not addressed by any expression within the sentence under evaluation—that is, in one sense of the term, it depends upon 'unarticulated constituents'. *If* the phenomenon of underarticulation is understood merely as addressing context-dependent aspects of an utterance's truth-conditions that are not accountable in terms of indexicality, then the view suggested in this chapter is indeed perfectly consonant with Crimmins and Perry's position.

Still, concessions on the antecedents of the foregoing conditionals grant precisely the point that this chapter aims to support. As for the relation between systems and intuitions, an account grounded on straightforward interpretive systems does not provide the premises needed for conclusions pertaining to the unreliability of our truth-conditional verdicts. That is, adapting Jonathan Berg's claim to the present case, belief reports do not at all support the 'startling claim' that 'competent speakers do not always know what they are saying' (Berg 2002: 354), and that they may systematically be mistaken with respect to a variety of everyday examples. As for Crimmins and Perry, nothing in the harmless understanding of underarticulation granted above supports dramatic conclusions pertaining to traditional interpretive systems' applicability to utterances of belief reports, and, more generally, to the limits of semantics and logic in this respect. To rephrase Crimmins and Perry's conclusion in a more appropriate vocabulary, the study of belief reports leaves quite a few doors open, or at least sufficiently ajar to allow for 'the simplest possible rules' of logical inference (see Crimmins and Perry 1989: 710).

6. *Where Am I Now?*

In this chapter, I proposed a simple interpretive system for languages equipped with the resources of attitude reports, and I explained why its results are compatible with our pre-theoretic intuitions of truth-conditions. Although I am sympathetic to the treatment of attitude reports in section 1, I did not devote this chapter to its direct defence: whether what I called 'straightforward assumptions' are indeed worthy of consideration is an issue on which I took no explicit position. My main aim, here as in the previous chapters of this book, has been to unveil the consequences of certain assumptions embedded in interpretive systems of the traditional type, pertaining to the relationships between meaning, truth, and the evaluation of particular utterances. Once these assumptions are properly understood, so I explained, the evidence provided by attitude reports does not entail any of the presumably unexpected theses which contemporary semanticists have been willing to entertain, and does not pose any problem for the conjunction of a simple 'Millian' take on proper names with other prima-facie plausible tenets.

Conclusion

IN this book, I have discussed the view of meaning and truth presupposed by what I called the 'traditional approach' to semantics, and I have analysed the extent to which it may be applied to particular instances of language use. The importance of these general issues is indirectly confirmed by the multitude of questions I confronted: I had something to say about the meaning of indexicals, the interpretation of 'messages recorded for later broadcast', the logic of indexicals, and discourse about fiction in Chapter 2; about the token-reflexive approach, the relationship between validity and utterability, the paradox of addressing, and approximations in Chapter 3; about contextualism, underarticulation, and semantic enrichment in Chapter 4; and about belief reports in Chapter 5.

Leaving aside my take on these particular problems, my general conclusion is not easily categorizable as falling within one or another of the alternative camps in the contemporary metasemantic debate. Of course, from the beginning I made no secret of the fact that I was approaching my topic with a sympathetic attitude towards the standard paradigm in natural language semantics. Still, I often found myself disagreeing with prominent defenders of the traditional standpoint, for a variety of different reasons. For instance, I took issue with David Kaplan's understanding of the logic of indexicals in Chapter 2, and with his arguments against token-reflexivity in Chapter 3. In Chapter 4 I explained my lack of enthusiasm for certain responses to contextualism typically put forth on behalf of the customary approach to semantics. And in Chapter 5 I remained unconvinced by the proposals defended by most of those who, like myself, seek a solution to the problem of belief reports within the scope of traditional interpretive systems.

My results are not merely negative. To the contrary, my criticism of this or that take on semantic analysis was intended to provide indirect support for what is hopefully a coherent and fruitful understanding of meaning, truth, and the use of language. In Chapter 2, for instance, I argued in favour of 'improper' indexes, and the logical consequences entailed by their acceptance within the system's structure. I also explained why the approach to meaning that accompanies a semantic treatment sympathetic to such indexes may be profitably employed in the analysis of a variety of phenomena, at least on a suitable understanding of the procedures governing the application of the system to particular examples. Questions of logic and application were also central in Chapter 3, where, among other things, I approached the puzzle of addressing and issues related to approximations. Finally, in Chapters 4 and 5, I suggested what I take to be the correct treatment of an important source of 'contextual variability', affecting examples such as my utterance of 'This is a vehicle' or your remarks on Tom's cognitive life.

When it comes to the issues particularly prominent in Chapter 4, the strategy I employed in favour of customary systems focuses on their intrinsic limitations: there is little point in demanding an analysis of an utterance's truth-conditions from structures that are not devised either to take utterances as their input or to yield truth-conditions as their output. Still, my focus on interpretive systems has helped me to maintain a healthy distance from the dogmatic stance characteristic of contemporary forms of anti-contextualism. All too often, philosophers intent on promoting the cause of the traditional view in the study of natural languages end up defending a peculiarly 'minimalist' approach to semantics, and a corresponding arbitrary isolation of the presumed semantic core from pragmatically contaminated considerations. If my view is on the right track, their commitment to a sterilized sense of truth-conditions and semantic content attaches an unnecessarily steep price to the traditional paradigm, and fuels the contextualists' distrust of an artificially shrinking sense of the scope of semantic inquiry.

The point is not that 'The leaves are green', 'This is a vehicle', or 'Tom believes that Dubya is the President' may not be uttered truly (or falsely, depending on one's preferred choice), and that our intuitions of truth (or falsehood) belong to the twilight zone of speaker meaning, pragmatic impartations, speech-act theory, or whatever name you care to give to 'the other side'. To the contrary, in my view, utterances of those sentences on different occasions may generate genuinely semantic contrasts, at least in a sense of semantics concerned with truth-conditions. Our intuitions, in other words, are indeed on the right track, and so-called pragmatic infiltrations do unquestionably contaminate an utterance's truth-conditional profile. Still, when it comes to the contribution provided by the interpretive system to the systematic analysis of an utterance's semantic properties, infiltrations of that type hardly affect the solidity of the traditional edifice: the relationship between the system's output and truth-conditions is, for very good reasons, a more sophisticated affair.

It is legitimate to complain that pruning the complexity of our intuitions for the sake of a favourite standpoint inevitably leads towards a barren theoretical landscape: an arid scenery lurks behind the minimalist mirage of an unspoiled semantic analysis. On the other hand, my insistence on the intrinsic boundaries of traditional interpretive systems steers clear of the risks of a 'semantics of the vacuum'. As explained in Chapter 1, there is an obvious and rather uncontroversial sense in which interpretive systems are not immediately applicable to particular utterances. That the system's semantic relevance is indirect also with respect to the system's output—that is, with respect to the relationship between truth-conditions and t-distributions—does not entail that interpretive systems are inevitably out of touch with semantic questions. To the contrary, the system's carefully calibrated interface with utterances and their truth-conditions provides the necessary background for its presentation of a particular theory of meaning, truth, and logic. It is a theory that, at least as far as the phenomena discussed in this book go, still deserves to occupy a central role in our approach to natural languages.

BIBLIOGRAPHY

Almog, J. (1986), 'Naming without Necessity', *Journal of Philosophy*, 83: 210–42.

Anderson, S. R., and Keenan, E. L. (1985), 'Deixis', in T. Shopen (ed.), *Language Typology and Syntactic Description, iii: Grammatical Categories and the Lexicon* (Cambridge: Cambridge University Press), 259–308.

Austin, J. L. (1961), 'The Meaning of a Word', in J. L. Austin, *Philosophical Papers*, ed. J. O. Urmson and G. J. Warnock (Oxford: Oxford University Press), 55–75; repr. in Caton (1963), 1–21.

Bach, K. (1992), 'Intentions and Demonstrations', *Analysis*, 52: 140–6.

—— (2000), 'Quantification, Qualification and Context: A Reply to Stanley and Szabó', *Mind and Language*, 15: 262–83.

Barwise, J., and Perry, J. (1983), *Situations and Attitudes* (Cambridge, Mass.: MIT Press).

Berg, J. (1988), 'The Pragmatics of Substitutivity', *Linguistics and Philosophy*, 11: 355–70.

—— (2002), 'Is Semantics Still Possible?', *Journal of Pragmatics*, 34: 349–59.

Bertolet, R. (1984), 'On a Fictional Ellipsis', *Erkenntnis*, 21: 189–94.

Bezuidenhout, A. (1996), 'Pragmatics and Singular Reference', *Mind and Language*, 11: 133–59.

—— (1997), 'Pragmatics, Semantics, Underdetermination and the Referential/Attributive Distinction', *Mind*, 106: 375–409.

Bianchi, C. (2001*a*), 'Context of Utterance and Intended Context', in V. Akman *et al.* (eds.), *Modeling and Using Context*, Proceedings of the Third International and Interdisciplinary Conference, CONTEXT '01, Dundee, Scotland (Berlin: Springer), 73–86.

—— (2001*b*), *La Dipendenza Contestuale: Per Una Teoria Pragmatica del Significato* (Naples: Edizioni Scientifiche Italiane).

Blackburn, S. (1984), *Spreading the Word: Groundings in the Philosophy of Language* (Oxford: Clarendon Press).

Blakemore, D. (2002), *Linguistic Meaning and Relevance: The Semantics and Pragmatics of Discourse Markers* (Cambridge: Cambridge University Press).

Borg, E. (2004), *How to Say What You Mean: Minimal Semantics and the Global Art of Communication* (Oxford: Oxford University Press).

—— (forthcoming), 'Saying What You Mean, Unarticulated Constituents and Communication', in R. Elugardo and R. Stainton (eds.), *Ellipsis and Non-Sentential Speech* (Dordrecht: Kluwer), 237–62.

Braun, D. (1994), 'Structured Characters and Complex Demonstratives', *Philosophical Studies*, 74: 193–219.

—— (1995), 'What is Character?', *Journal of Philosophical Logic*, 24: 227–40.

—— (1996), 'Demonstratives and their Linguistic Meaning', *Nous*, 30: 145–73.

—— (1998), 'Understanding Belief Reports', *Philosophical Review*, 107: 555–95.

Caplan, B. (2003), 'Putting things in Context', *Philosophical Review*.

Carston, R. (1988), 'Implicature, Explicature, and Truth-Theoretic Semantics', in R. Kempson (ed.), *Mental Representations* (Cambridge: Cambridge University Press), 155–79.

—— (2002), *Thoughts and Utterances: The Pragmatics of Explicit Communication* (Oxford: Blackwell).

—— (forthcoming), 'Explicature and Semantics', in S. Davis and B. Gillon (eds.), *Semantics: A Reader* (Oxford: Oxford University Press).

Caton, C. E. (1963) (ed.), *Philosophy and Ordinary Language* (Chicago: University of Illinois Press).

Clapp, L. (1995), 'How to be Direct and Innocent: A Criticism of Crimmins and Perry's Theory of Attitude Ascriptions', *Linguistics and Philosophy*, 18: 529–65.

Colterjohn, J., and MacIntosh, D. (1987), 'Gerald Vision and Indexicals', *Analysis*, 47: 58–60.

Corazza, E. (2003), 'Thinking the Unthinkable: An Excursion into Z-Land', in M. O'Rourke and C. Washington (eds.), *Situating Semantics: Essays on the Philosophy of John Perry* (Cambridge, Mass.: MIT Press).

—— (2004), 'On the Alleged Ambiguity of "Now" and "Here"', *Synthese*, 138: 289–313.

—— Fish, W., and Gorvett, J. (2002), 'Who Is I?', *Philosophical Studies*, 107: 1–21.

Crimmins, M. (1992a), 'Context in Attitudes', *Linguistics and Philosophy*, 15: 185–98.

—— (1992b), *Talk About Beliefs* (Cambridge, Mass.: MIT Press).

—— (1993), 'So-Labeled Neofregeanism', *Philosophical Studies*, 69: 265–79.

—— (1995), 'Contextuality, Reflexivity, Iteration, Logic', *Philosophical Perspectives*, 9: 381–99.

—— and Perry, J. (1989), 'The Prince and the Phone Booth, Reporting Puzzling Beliefs', *Journal of Philosophy*, 86: 685–711.

Crossley, J. N., and Humberstone, L. (1977), 'The Logic of "Actually" ', *Reports on Mathematical Logic*, 8: 11–29.

Crystal, D. (1991), *A Dictionary of Linguistics and Phonetics*, 3rd edn. (Oxford: Blackwell).

Davidson, D. (1984), *Inquiries into Truth and Interpretation* (Oxford: Clarendon Press).

Devitt, M. (1981), *Designation* (New York: Columbia University Press).

Dowty, D. R., Wall, R. E., and Peters, S. (1981), *Introduction to Montague Semantics* (Dordrecht: D. Reidel Publishing Company).

Field, H. (1973), 'Theory Change and the Indeterminacy of Reference', *Journal of Philosophy*, 70: 462–81.

Fillmore, C. (1975), *Santa Cruz Lectures on Deixis 1971*, reproduced by the Indiana University Linguistic Club.

Forbes, G. (1990), 'The Indispensability of *Sinn*', *Philosophical Review*, 99: 535–64.

—— (1993), 'Reply to Marks', *Philosophical Studies*, 69: 281–95.

Frege, G. (1892), 'On *Sinn* and *Bedeutung*', in M. Beaney (ed.), *The Frege Reader* (Oxford: Blackwell), 151–71.

—— (1914), 'Logic in Mathematics', in G. Frege, *Posthumous Writings* (Oxford: Blackwell), 201–50.

Garcia-Carpintero, M. (1998), 'Indexicals as Token-Reflexives', *Mind*, 107: 529–63.

—— (2000), 'Token-Reflexivity and Indirect Discourse', in A. Kanamori (ed.), *The Proceedings of the Twentieth World Congress of Philosophy*, vi: *Analytic Philosophy and Logic* (Bowling Green, Oh.: Philosophy Documentation Center), 37–56.

Gauker, C. (1997a), 'Domain of Discourse', *Mind*, 106: 1–32.

—— (1997b), 'Universal Instantiation: A Study of the Role of Context in Logic', *Erkenntnis*, 46: 185–214.

—— (1998), 'What is a Context of Utterance?', *Philosophical Studies*, 91: 149–72.

Gorvett, J. (forthcoming), 'Back through the Looking Glass: On the Relationship between Intentions and Indexicals', *Philosophical Studies*.

Hildesheimer, W. (1982), *Mozart* (New York: Noonday Press).

Kamp, H., and Reyle, U. (1993), *From Discourse to Logic* (Dordrecht: Kluwer Academic Publishers).

Kaplan, D. (1977), 'Demonstratives', in J. Almog, J. Perry, and H. Wettstein (eds.), *Themes from Kaplan* (New York and Oxford: Oxford University Press, 1989), 481–563.

—— (1989), 'Afterthoughts', in J. Almog, J. Perry, and H. Wettstein (eds.), *Themes from Kaplan* (New York and Oxford: Oxford University Press, 1989), 565–614.

—— (1990), 'Words', *Proceedings of the Aristotelian Society*, suppl. vol. 64: 93–119.

Kripke, S. (1972), *Naming and Necessity* (Cambridge, Mass.: Harvard University Press).

—— (1979), 'A Puzzle about Belief', in A. Margalit (ed.), *Meaning and Use* (Dordrecht: Reidel), 239–83; repr. in N. Salmon and S. Soames (eds.), *Propositions and Attitudes* (Oxford: Oxford University Press, 1988), 102–48.

Lahav, R. (1989), 'Against Compositionality: The Case of Adjectives', *Philosophical Studies*, 57: 261–79.

Levinson, S. C. (2000), *Presumptive Meanings: The Theory of Generalized Conversational Implicature* (Cambridge, Mass.: MIT Press).

Lewis, D. (1970), 'Anselm and Actuality', *Nous*, 4: 175–88; repr. in Lewis (1983), 10–26.

—— (1978), 'Truth in Fiction', *American Philosophical Quarterly*, 15: 37–46.

—— (1979), 'Scorekeeping in a Language Game', *Journal of Philosophical Logic*, 8: 339–59; repr. in Lewis (1983), 233–49.

—— (1980), 'Index, Context, and Content', in S. Kanger and S. Öhman (eds.), *Philosophy and Grammar* (Dordrecht: Reidel); repr. in D. Lewis, *Papers in Philosophical Logic* (Cambridge: Cambridge University Press, 1998), 21–44.

—— (1983), *Philosophical Papers, i* (Oxford: Oxford University Press).

Ludlow, P. (1995), 'Logical Form and the Hidden-Indexical Theory: A Reply to Schiffer', *Journal of Philosophy*, 92: 102–7.

—— (1996), 'The Adicity of "Believes" and the Hidden Indexical Theory', *Analysis*, 56: 97–101.

Marti, G. (2003), 'The Question of Rigidity in New Theories of Reference', *Nous*, 37: 161–79.

Montague, R. (1968), 'Pragmatics', in R. Klibansky (ed.), *Contemporary Philosophy—La philosophie contemporaine* (Florence: La Nuova Italia Editrice), 102–22.

Neale, S. (1992), 'Paul Grice and the Philosophy of Language', *Linguistics and Philosophy*, 15: 509–59.

—— (2000), 'On Being Explicit: Comments on Stanley and Szabó, and on Bach', *Mind and Language*, 15: 284–94.

Partee, B. (1989), 'Binding Implicit Variables in Quantified Contexts', *CLS* 25.

Perry, J. (1986), 'Thought without Representation', *Proceedings of the Aristotelian Society*, suppl. vol. 60: 137–52.

—— (1997), 'Indexicals and Demonstratives', in R. Hale and C. Wright (eds.), *A Companion to the Philosophy of Language* (Oxford: Blackwell), 586–612.

—— (1998a), 'Indexicals, Contexts and Unarticulated Constituents', in *Proceedings of the 1995 CSLI-Amsterdam Logic, Language and Computation Conference* (Stanford, Calif.: CSLI Publications), 1–16.

—— (1998b), 'Myself and I', in M. Stamm (ed.), *Philosophie in Synthetischer Absicht* (Stuttgart: Klett-Cotta), 83–103; repr. in J. Perry, *The Problem of the Essential Indexical and Other Essays* (Stanford, Calif.: CSLI Publications), 325–39.

—— (2001), *Reference and Reflexivity* (Stanford, Calif.: CSLI Publications).

—— (2003), 'Predelli's Threatening Note: Contexts, Utterances, and Token in the Philosophy of Language', *Journal of Pragmatics*, 35: 373–87.

Predelli, S. (1996), 'Never Put Off Until Tomorrow What You Can Do Today', *Analysis*, 56: 85–91.

—— (1997), 'Talk about Fiction', *Erkenntnis*, 46: 69–77.

—— (1998), 'I Am Not Here Now', *Analysis*, 58: 107–15.

—— (2001), 'Names and Character', *Philosophical Studies*, 103: 145–63.

—— (2002a), ' "Holmes" and Holmes: A Millian Analysis of Names from Fiction', *Dialectica*, 56: 261–79.

—— (2002b), 'Intentions, Indexicals, and Communication', *Analysis*, 62: 310–16.

—— (2004), 'Semantic Contextuality', *Journal of Pragmatics*, 36: 2107–23.

—— (forthcoming), 'The Lean Mean Semantic Machine', in C. Bianchi (ed.), *The Semantics/Pragmatics Distinction* (Stanford, Calif.: CSLI Publications).

Quine, W. V. O. (1953), 'Mr. Strawson on Logical Theory', *Mind*, 62: 433–51; repr. in W. V. O. Quine, *The Ways of Paradox and Other Essays*, rev. enlarged edn. (Cambridge, Mass.: Harvard University Press), 137–57.

—— (1960), *Word and Object* (Cambridge, Mass.: MIT Press).

Recanati, F. (1993), *Direct Reference: From Language to Thought* (Oxford: Blackwell).

—— (2001), 'What Is Said', *Synthese*, 128: 75–91.

—— (2002a), 'Deixis and Anaphora', in Z. Szabó (ed.), *Semantics vs. Pragmatics* (Oxford: Oxford University Press).

—— (2002b), 'Pragmatics and Semantics', in L. Horn and G. Ward (eds.), *Handbook of Pragmatics* (Oxford: Blackwell).

—— (2002c), 'Unarticulated Constituents', *Linguistics and Philosophy*, 25: 299–345.

—— (2003), *Literal Meaning* (Cambridge, Mass.: MIT Press).

Reichenbach, H. (1947), *Elements of Symbolic Logic* (New York: Free Press).

Reimer, M. (1991a), 'Demonstratives, Demonstrations, and Demonstrata', *Philosophical Studies*, 63: 187–202.

—— (1991b), 'Do Demonstrations Have Semantic Significance?', *Analysis*, 51: 177–83.

Richard, M. (1981), 'Temporalism and Eternalism', *Philosophical Studies*, 39: 1–13.

—— (1982), 'Tense, Propositions, and Meanings', *Philosophical Studies*, 41: 337–51.

—— (1990), *Propositional Attitudes: An Essay on Thoughts and How We Ascribe Them* (Cambridge: Cambridge University Press).

—— (1993), 'Attitudes in Context', *Linguistics and Philosophy*, 16: 123–48.

—— (1995), 'Defective Contexts, Accommodation, and Normalization', *Canadian Journal of Philosophy*, 25: 551–70.

Riegert, R. (1990), *California: The Ultimate Guidebook* (Berkeley: Ulysses Press).

Robbins Landon, H. C. (1988), *1791 Mozart's Last Year* (New York: Schirmer Books).

Romdenh-Romluc, K. (2002), 'Now the French are Invading England!', *Analysis*, 62: 34–41.

Sainsbury, M. (2001), 'Two Ways to Smoke a Cigarette', *Ratio*, 14: 386–406.

Salmon, N. (1986), *Frege's Puzzle* (Cambridge, Mass.: MIT Press).

—— (1987), 'Existence', *Philosophical Perspectives*, 1: 49–108.

—— (1989), 'Illogical Belief', *Philosophical Perspectives*, 3: 243–85.

—— (1991), 'How *Not* to Become a Millian Heir', *Philosophical Studies*, 62: 165–77.

—— (1995), 'Being of Two Minds: Belief with Doubt', *Nous*, 29: 1–20.

Salmon, N. (1998), 'Nonexistence', *Nous*, 32: 277–319.

Santambrogio, M. (2002), 'Belief and Translation', *Journal of Philosophy*, 99: 624–47.

Saul, J. (1993), 'Still an Attitude Problem', *Linguistics and Philosophy*, 16: 423–35.

—— (1998), 'The Pragmatics of Attitude Ascription', *Philosophical Studies*, 92: 363–89.

—— (2002a), 'Speaker Meaning, What is Said, and What is Implicated', *Nous*, 36: 228–48.

—— (2002b), 'What is Said and Psychological Reality: Grice's Project and Relevance Theorists' Criticisms', *Linguistics and Philosophy*, 25: 347–72.

Schiffer, S. (1990), 'The Relational Theory of Belief [A Reply to Mark Richard]', *Pacific Philosophical Quarterly*, 71: 240–5.

—— (1992), 'Belief Ascription', *Journal of Philosophy*, 89: 499–521.

—— (1996), 'The Hidden-Indexical Theory's Logical Form Problem: A Rejoinder', *Analysis*, 56: 92–7.

Schlenker, P. (2004), 'Context of Thought and Context of Utterance: A Note on Free Indirect Discourse and the Historical Present', *Mind and Language*, 19: 279–304.

Searle, J. R. (1980), 'The Background of Meaning', in J. R. Searle, F. Kiefer, and M. Bierwisch (eds.), *Speech Act Theory and Pragmatics* (Dordrecht: D. Reidel Publishing Company), 221–32.

Sidelle, A. (1991), 'The Answering Machine Paradox', *Canadian Journal of Philosophy*, 21: 525–39.

Sider, T. (1995), 'Three Problems for Richard's Theory of Belief Ascription', *Canadian Journal of Philosophy*, 25: 487–513.

Smith, Q. (1989), 'The Multiple Uses of Indexicals', *Synthese*, 78: 167–91.

Soames, S. (1987a), 'Direct Reference, Propositional Attitudes, and Semantic Content', *Philosophical Topics*, 15: 47–87.

—— (1987b), 'Substitutivity', in J. J. Thomson (ed.), *On Being and Saying: Essays for Richard Cartwright* (Cambridge, Mass.: MIT Press), 99–132.

—— (1995), 'Beyond Singular Propositions?', *Canadian Journal of Philosophy*, 25: 515–50.

Sperber, D., and Wilson, D. (1995), *Relevance: Communication and Cognition*, 2nd edn. (Oxford: Blackwell).

Stanley, J. (2000), 'Context and Logical Form', *Linguistics and Philosophy*, 23: 391–434.

—— (2002a), 'Making it Articulated', *Mind and Language*, 17: 149–68.

—— (2002b), 'Nominal Restriction', in G. Peters and G. Preyer (eds.), *Logical Form and Language* (Oxford: Oxford University Press), 365–88.

—— and Szabó, Z. G. (2000a), 'On Quantifier Domain Restriction', *Mind and Language*, 15: 216–61.

—— —— (2000b), 'Reply to Bach and Neale', *Mind and Language*, 15: 295–8.

Storto, G. (2002), 'Possessives in Context', MS.

Strawson, P. (1952), *Introduction to Logical Theory* (London: Methuen).

Szabó, Z. G. (2001), 'Adjectives in Context', in I. Kenesei and R. M. Harnish (eds.), *Perspectives on Semantics, Pragmatics, and Discourse: A Festschrift for Ferenc Kiefer* (Amsterdam: John Benjamins Publishing Company).

Taylor, K. A. (2001), 'Sex, Breakfast, and Descriptus-Interruptus', *Synthese*, 128: 45–61.

Travis, C. (1985), 'On What is Strictly Speaking True', *Canadian Journal of Philosophy*, 15: 187–229.

—— (1989), *The Uses of Sense: Wittgenstein's Philosophy of Language* (Oxford: Clarendon Press).

—— (1996), 'Meaning's Role in Truth', *Mind*, 105: 451–66.

—— (1997), 'Pragmatics', in B. Hale and C. Wright (eds.), *A Companion to the Philosophy of Language* (Oxford: Blackwell), 87–107.

Tsohatzidis, S. L. (1992), 'Pronouns of Address and Truth Conditions', *Linguistics*, 30: 569–75.

Vision, G. (1985), 'I Am Here Now', *Analysis*, 45: 198–9.

Wachtel, T. (1980), 'Pragmatic Approximations', *Journal of Pragmatics*, 4: 201–11.

Wettstein, H. (1986), 'Has Semantics Rested on a Mistake?', *Journal of Philosophy*, 83: 185–209.

Wilson, D., and Sperber, D. (1981), 'On Grice's Theory of Conversation', in P. Werth (ed.), *Conversation and Discourse: Structure and Interpretation* (London: Croom Helm), 155–78.

Zimmermann, T. (1997), 'The Addressing Puzzle', in W. Künne, A. Newen, and M. Anduschus (eds.), *Direct Reference, Indexicality, and Propositional Attitudes* (Stanford, Calif.: CSLI Publications), 133–53.

INDEX

addressing (puzzle of) 109–11
approximations 111–16
attitude reports 7, 161–74, 177–82
Austin, J. L. 120, 123

Bach, K. 25, 135
Berg, J. 131, 133, 163, 182
Bezuidenhout, A. 31, 33, 125
Bianchi, C. 54, 128
Borg, E. 131–2
Braun, D. 21, 163

Carston, R. 30, 33–4, 122–5, 128, 130, 147
character 20–1, 45–9
clause 3–5, 14–18, 23–5, 66–9, 116, 134–5
Colterjohn, J. 47–9
contextualism 6, 29–38, 119–29
Corazza, E. 44, 54, 58, 156
Crimmins, M. 78, 106, 156–8, 162–3, 170, 181–2

fiction (discourse about) 66–73
Forbes, G. 106, 162

Frege, G. 122–4, 162

Garcia-Carpintero, M. 78, 80–1, 90
Gauker, C. 24, 116

index, indexical 2–5, 17–20, 23, 32–8, 41–6, 53–66, 69–73, 80–2, 86–8, 93–104, 106–16, 134–5
interpretive system 3–4, 11–33, 58–66, 164–8

Kamp, H. 2, 15, 54
Kaplan, D. 2, 20, 23, 25, 30–2, 37, 46, 55, 60–2, 64–5, 74, 76–9, 83, 89–92, 95, 99, 102–3, 166.
Kripke, S. 166, 168.

Levinson, S. 31, 33
Lewis, D. 18, 23, 32, 67–8, 70, 115, 137

MacIntosh, D. 47–9
Montague, R. 31–2, 122

Neale, S. 30, 135

Perry, J. 12, 44, 78, 80, 155–8, 163, 181–2

Quine, W. V. O. 28–9, 32, 58, 106, 152

Recanati, F. 35–7, 54, 74–5, 122–5, 128, 147, 158, 166
Reichenbach, H. 77–8
Reimer, M. 25, 163
Richard, M. 12, 130, 163

Salmon, N. 46, 70, 73, 106, 163, 166, 181
Saul, J. 132, 163, 172
Searle, J. 119, 174, 176
semantics (traditional) 1–2, 8–11, 149–54, 161–4, 184–7
Sidelle, A. 49–53, 60

Smith, Q. 46, 49, 57, 151–2
Soames, S. 163, 181
Sperber, D. 29–3, 125
Strawson, P. 28, 133

t-distribution 3–4, 6, 12–13, 19–20, 138–49, 174–7
token-reflexivity 5, 76–102
Travis, C. 119–20, 123–5, 127–8, 131, 135, 147
truth-conditions 4, 6, 130–3, 136–49, 174–7

underarticulation 127, 154–9
utterance 3–4, 49–53, 60–2, 105–16
utterance, representation of 3–4, 23–7, 40–6, 53–8, 66–73, 93–8

Wilson, D. 29–30, 33, 125